CROSS-BORDER GIVING

A LEGAL AND PRACTICAL GUIDE

CONTRIBUTING AUTHORS

John Bennett
Victoria Bjorklund
Betsy Brill
Heather Grady
Kay Guinane
Nancy Herzog
Beth Kingsley
Jessie Krafft

Amanda MacArthur
Jane Peebles
Adam Pickering
David Pritchard
Patricia Rosenfield
David Shevlin
Deirdre White
Susan Winer

EDITED BY

Ted Hart and Kinga Ile

Cross-Border Giving: A Legal and Practical Guide

Published by
CharityChannel Press, an imprint of CharityChannel LLC
424 Church Street, Suite 2000
Nashville, TN 37219 USA

CharityChannel.com

ISBN Print Book: 978-1-938077-93-7

Library of Congress Control Number: 2018936036

13 12 11 10 9 8 7 6 5 4 3 2 1

Printed in the United States of America

This and most CharityChannel Press books are available at special quantity discounts for bulk purchases for sales promotions, premiums, fundraising, or educational use. For information, contact CharityChannel Press, 424 Church Street, Suite 2000, Nashville, TN 37219 USA. +1 949-589-5938.

Publisher's Acknowledgments

This book was produced by a team dedicated to excellence; please send your feedback to Editors@CharityChannel.com.

We first wish to acknowledge the tens of thousands of peers who call *CharityChannel.com* their online professional home. Your enthusiastic support for CharityChannel Press is the wind in our sails.

Members of the team who produced this book include:

Editors

Acquisitions: Linda Lysakowski

Manuscript Editing: Stephen Nill

Production

Cover: Ron Crognale, CAF America

Layout: Jill McLain

Administrative

CharityChannel LLC: Stephen Nill, CEO

Marketing and Public Relations: John Millen

Dedication

CAF America dedicates this book to those who believe in the power of international philanthropy and to those who wish to learn from decades of best practices from the foremost experts in the field. Your tireless commitment to making a difference transcends borders and it brings about change where it is most needed.

Editors' Acknowledgments

This book is the result of a collaborative effort by acclaimed professionals selected by CAF America for their expertise and practical insights on the complex world of international philanthropy. As the editors, we want *Cross-Border Giving: A Legal and Practical Guide* to be a resource for those who are committed to making a difference through regulatory compliant strategic international philanthropy.

We would like to acknowledge and thank our contributing authors for enthusiastically taking on this project in addition to your full-time professional roles. You have delivered in-depth regulatory analysis and shared best practices, lessons learned, and tips that will greatly benefit our readers. We also appreciate your receptivity to our edits and strict deadlines. We enjoyed working with each and every one of you.

Thank you, also, to the editorial team at CharityChannel Press, Stephen Nill, Jill McLain, and Linda Lysakowski, for their expert publishing guidance throughout every phase of this undertaking. Their immense dedication and editorial support made the publishing of *Cross-Border Giving: A Legal and Practical Guide* a successful journey. Your consistent availability, punctuality, and attention to detail was vital to the success of this book.

It is our pleasure to acknowledge the hard work of all our colleagues at CAF America, who provided their expertise to and support of our research, editing, and formatting, as well as designing the book cover. While many members of the staff helped, we owe a great deal to the individual efforts of Brian Kastner, Officer of Thought Leadership, and Ron Crognale, Director of Communications.

Contents

Comments from the Field

This important reference will help experienced and new grantmakers, organizations seeking US-based donors, and anyone seeking a deeper impact with their giving. The regulations for international giving can be daunting; this book brings clarity and cuts through the confusion. I highly recommend it.

Dr. Melissa A. Berman
President & CEO
Rockefeller Philanthropy Advisors

If you are a philanthropist working in international development, this publication is for you. It offers an excellent overview of the recent philanthropy and development trends and illustrates how to link action and impact.

Karolina Mzyk Callias
Programme Specialist in UNDP and a Global Team Leader
SDG Philanthropy Platform

This book brings CAF America's deep expertise, experience, and relationships in cross-border grantmaking to a wide audience, providing international investment portfolios the confidence to build the workforce of tomorrow and drive innovative global solutions to address the world's most pressing challenges.

Rob Vallentine
Director, Global Citizenship, The Dow Chemical Company
President, The Dow Chemical Company Foundation

Introduction

Understanding the 3Rs of Successful Cross-Border Giving

Ted Hart

Donors from the United States are known around the world for their generosity. A record-breaking $390.05 billion was given by US donors to charities in 2016 as highlighted by the Giving USA 2017 Report.[1] The number of foundations, corporations, and individuals committed to advancing philanthropy beyond the borders of the United States is rapidly growing, with gifts to the international affairs subsector growing to represent the seventh-largest share of charitable dollars across the landscape for US charitable giving. However, these donors often face daunting challenges. Complex US and international regulatory frameworks apply to cross-border giving, and a lack of understanding of these rules and regulations can result in excessive exposure of donors to risks impacting both their bank accounts and their reputation. In this age of increased prevalence of money laundering, terrorist financing, and an ongoing global trend of tightening regulation of the nonprofit sector, compliance in cross-border grantmaking has never been more difficult nor more important to achieve.

Even with the noblest of intentions and goals, if donors do not ensure that their funding is going to well vetted, trustworthy recipients they could be doing more harm than good. As you will learn from the authors in this book, many issues must be addressed when US donors, be they

---

[1] Giving USA Foundation, *Giving USA 2017: The Annual Report on Philanthropy for the Year 2016* (Chicago: Giving USA Foundation, 2017), *givingusa.org/tag/giving-usa-2017*.

foundations, individuals, corporations, or anyone else involved in philanthropy, choose to make cross-border donations. These span a wide range of regulatory compliance issues, such as adhering to laws blocking the use of charitable funds to finance organized crime and terrorism, preventing the cooptation of the grantmaking process for fraud or personal gain, and ensuring full compliance with applicable laws in the foreign countries that host grant beneficiaries.

CAF America has worked with these expert authors to develop a comprehensive and practical guide discussing the challenges, reviewing best practices, and providing case study examples of cross-border giving. The contributing authors have been selected because they are leaders in their field, masters not only of the underlying theory but also of the day-to-day implementation of expertly designed policies and procedures. They are therefore well positioned to share lessons learned and tips for best practice.

The 3Rs of International Grantmaking

When compared to domestic giving, the regulations and best practices that contribute to successful grantmaking across borders are much more complex with increased chances of unwittingly running afoul of regulators and tax authorities. Compliance with the large body of regulations, both US and foreign, is the most complicated and (understandably) one of the most intimidating concern for grantmakers looking to support foreign nonprofits.

Compliance with US *regulations (the first R)* is often only part of the equation; grantmakers must also be aware of international regulations as well as those established by *each country* related to successfully moving granted funds to local charities and projects. Failure to comply with US laws carries the *risk (the second R)* of significant excise taxes and fines, or even criminal charges. In the case of foundations making the grant themselves, they could face revocation of 501(c)(3) status, depending on the law that has been violated. Ignoring foreign laws may result in (among others) the suspension or blacklisting of your organization from operating in a foreign country, seizure of the granted funds, and can greatly jeopardize the operations of your grantees who would also be exposed to potentially serious penalties. In addition to the myriad of legal concerns grantmakers face, they must also be concerned about their (and, if applicable, their donors') *reputation (the third R)*. Reputational damage could have devastating consequences for you or your organization's future charitable activities.

These three main concerns—regulatory compliance, risk management, and reputation protection—form the blueprint for a coherent, strategic, and, most importantly, successful approach to international grantmaking.

Regulatory Compliance

There is a complicated matrix of US and foreign regulations governing cross-border giving; as a result, your compliance protocols will need to be concentrated on several key areas of grantmaker responsibility. The first, and most important, aspect of tax-effective charitable giving revolves around the strictures of the Internal Revenue Code (IRC) for the establishment of a grantee's charitable purpose. There are two established and increasingly well-defined tools and processes for doing this: equivalency determination (commonly known as ED) and expenditure responsibility (commonly known as ER).

Following the September 11, 2001 terrorist attacks, both the US government and the United Nations (as well as many other nations around the world) have implemented new regimes of international enforcement to fight the proliferation of money laundering, terrorist financing, and organized crime. Because foreign grantee organizations can sometimes operate in delicate or high-risk countries, the responsibility for determining that they are not involved in illicit activities falls squarely on you, the grantmaker. Additionally, it would not be wise to assume—just because you are funding a charity in a more developed part of the world—that these regulations do not apply to your organization. Your vetting procedures must be sufficiently robust to ensure that you and the nonprofit or project receiving your funding are compliant with all regulations. Not knowing about the regulations is no excuse in the eyes of regulators.

Increasingly, many countries around the world are enacting stringent restrictions on nonprofits that can make it challenging for them to accept funding from foreign sources. There is a concerning global trend—often referred to as *the closing space for civil society*—that threatens nonprofits' independence and, by extension, their existence. Whether motivated by the local government's intention to conduct closer monitoring of foreign funding with the aim of fighting money laundering and terrorist activities, or part of a wider initiative of a government targeting their country's nonprofit sector for the possible purpose of silencing voices of opposition, grantmakers must be cognizant and proactive in adhering to these laws when granting internationally in order to avoid exposing your grantees to unnecessary risks.

Risk Management

Giving internationally could make your organization a high-profile target for individuals and groups looking to launder money simply for tax avoidance or in support of organized criminal activities like terrorism or trafficking. You might also think the grantee is capable or wishes to comply with the terms of your grant only to find the organization has failed to account for the use of the funds or the funds have been stolen. It is therefore essential to employ a very detailed risk-based vetting regimen for your potential grantees. Consistent and comprehensive due diligence is your best means of managing risk.

Know Your Customer standards required of the banking sector provide important guidelines for grantmakers who may work on behalf of other donors, whether they may be individuals, foundations, or corporations. Adhering to federal guidance on these procedures—including the US Department of the Treasury's Voluntary Guidelines for International Grantmaking—can significantly reduce your exposure to the risks involved.[2]

Only give to organizations you know well and have fully vetted, or have been fully vetted on your behalf by a third party you trust and has a track record for strong due diligence and successful international grantmaking.

Reputation Protection

One grant made wrong can result in a public fine, one grant made to a poorly vetted organization could end up with monies being funneled to terrorists, one grant made to a poorly-managed organization might be stolen, one grant made to an organization whose governance structure

---

[2] See **Chapter Nine** for more details on Voluntary Guidelines.

does not comply with best practices risks funds being mismanaged. Just one story in the press can ruin the reputation of the donor, the corporation, or the foundation making the grant.

Every organization involved in international grantmaking must be concerned with protecting its reputation. As organizations that serve and benefit from the public's trust, nonprofits are subject to the court of public opinion. One bad grant can have devastating consequences for the organization, its donors, and its grantees.

Being associated with organized crime, terrorism, or having low standards for due diligence will severely impact your ability to further your philanthropic mission.

It is through the consistent deployment of deep due diligence and regulatory compliance regimes that you can best guarantee compliance, remove the risk inherent to international grantmaking and protect your reputation and that of your grantees. By maintaining a focus on these three aspects of cross-border grantmaking, you will define an approach to international philanthropy that results in the best possible support for nonprofits and charitable causes around the world.

Ten Questions You Must Ask of an International Grantmaking Intermediary Before You Sign the Agreement

Due to the complexity of cross-border grantmaking, it is common for donors—whether corporations, foundations or individuals—to engage the services of an international grantmaking intermediary. This can be a very good way to ensure regulatory compliance, manage risk, and protect your reputation. To assist you in making a well-informed decision, we have assembled ten important questions the intermediary must answer to your satisfaction before you sign any agreement. This book will help you understand what an accurate and reliable answer is, and what is not.

1. What are the fees charged for the services you require? Are there additional fees for granting to high-risk areas? What services are included in the quoted fees and what additional fees might be incurred?

2. In how many countries has the intermediary successfully vetted organizations and made grants? Can you advise gifts to the organization of your choice, or only to a list of prescribed organizations?

3. What is the longevity and experience of the intermediary? How many years of successful international grantmaking do they have? What is the intermediary's reputation internationally and in the places where it supports projects?

4. Does the intermediary vet the organization they grant to or are they relying on the advice of others? If so whom? And why? What happens if the organization of your choice fails to become approved (vetted) by the intermediary?

5. What protocol does the intermediary use to vet foreign organizations? Quiz the intermediary on their understanding of US and international regulations related to ED, ER, AML, FATF, OFAC, FCPA, USA PATRIOT Act, and CFT.

6. Does the intermediary take full risk and responsibility for the grant being made or do they shift the risk to you? Are they fully aware of the laws governing the transfer of your donation into the foreign country?

7. What controls does the intermediary have in place to ensure that funds are spent effectively?

8. Does the intermediary have offices and experts around the world who can assist in grantmaking or are they relying only on the internet or single office staff?

9. Does the intermediary also support domestic giving? How are grants transmitted to foreign organizations (wire transfer, physical check, etc.)?

10. Does the intermediary have 501(c)(3) status in the US? If not, are you comfortable with knowing that you won't receive tax benefits as a result of your donation?

Cultural Challenges of Working with Foreign Grantees: A Case Study from Bulgaria

Following the 3Rs will greatly improve your likelihood of having success in making grants internationally. However, there are additional challenges that you may face. The experience of working with the Helen L. Rinker Ashley Fund at CAF America illustrates some of the unique cultural challenges that can be inherent to international grantmaking, and solutions we developed with our implementing partner.

The Case of Voditsa Bulgaria

Helen L. Rinker Ashley came to CAF America as a client before I began serving as President and CEO, wishing to establish a fund to benefit the people of a small village in Bulgaria located in the Popovo Municipality in Targovishte Province, Northeastern Bulgaria, a village named Voditsa. As we learned, Mrs. Rinker Ashley's parents had lived there their entire life, and having other family ties with the village she continued to visit often. In the founding documents of the donor advised fund (DAF) she opened at CAF America, she advised that her legacy gift should support infrastructure development and contribute to the education of the children in Voditsa. We received her intended contribution to the DAF from her estate upon Mrs. Rinker Ashley's passing in 2011.

The first step was to communicate with the village that a fund had been established and to begin the due diligence and planning process needed to fulfill her advised wishes. My predecessor traveled to Bulgaria and very publicly announced that Voditsa was the recipient of a large legacy gift.

Upon evaluation, it was apparent that Voditsa lacked a nonprofit community that could carry out the types of infrastructure projects envisioned by Mrs. Rinker Ashley. With such advice from the donor, it is our preference to help build the local economy by partnering with local nonprofits, who would themselves implement the projects and to whom we could directly grant money as long as they could be validated by our staff as eligible to receive grants from US donors. This was decidedly not the case in tiny Voditsa. In many countries, you will find that small communities either do not have a very strong civil society infrastructure, or have one that is highly concentrated around the country's capital, or are in periods of transition in which local nonprofits are unorganized or informal. To ensure that our activities could fit within the framework of US and Bulgarian regulations, the decision was made to partner with the Sofia-based Bulgarian organization known as BCause Foundation (BCause). BCause served as our grantee and the agreement provided for that organization to implement charitable projects in Voditsa on behalf of CAF America.

Soon after the public announcement was made, village residents began calling BCause asking where their money was and why it was being kept from them. When we learned of this, we were, of course, concerned there had been a misunderstanding; and there had been. Raising an important issue in successful international grantmaking, that of cultural sensitivity.

The problem, as it turned out, stemmed from the fact that in Bulgarian, the words *legacy gift* translated as a term more similar to *inheritance*. The people in Voditsa initially had completely different expectations for these funds and their subsequent disbursement than was the intended purpose. As you may know, regulations governing the use of DAFs forbid the disbursement of funds to individuals, and Mrs. Rinker Ashley had advised her gift for specific purposes that did not include disbursements to individuals. So regulatory compliance (see the 3Rs) and this cultural stress point created an unfortunate disconnect between CAF America's obligations and the villagers' expectations. This led to tensions between the village and BCause, even allegations of potential theft (though no funds had been disbursed), and a general breakdown of trust between all parties.

To protect our reputation and that of our partner organization, BCause brought in external consultants to facilitate discussions with the community. It was vital to have third party representatives present in the community to explain the regulations and processes governing the disbursement of the grant. It took many months to bridge the cultural divide, but thankfully this strategy eventually led to a rebuilding of trust between the community, BCause, and CAF America. At the end of this process, the villagers were reassured that the money was not being withheld for inappropriate reasons—creating a fundamental understanding that predicated the project's success.

After mutual understanding was achieved, CAF America and BCause could begin with the implementation work itself. In this, we encountered another roadblock: our Bulgarian beneficiaries, and the other organizations that we worked with in the country, were not familiar with the types of projects that could be funded under section 501(c)(3) of the IRC, which defines charitable purpose. This prompted concerns about risk (see the 3Rs), and while we received many grant applications for ideas such as large infrastructure projects and vague community development initiatives, we needed to understand the risks we could face in funding an ill-defined project that we could not clearly show to be charitable.

Again, this pointed to a common problem often faced when funding charitable projects outside the United States. While many of us have a general knowledge (and this book will help you gain a much higher level of knowledge) of what is charitable and what is not, there was a lack of understanding within the village of what was meant by various phrases, and it became clear that our application process was not clarifying the matter but was instead adding to the confusion. This example is not to suggest that our partners and or the villagers were to blame for these difficulties—they were simply not experienced in receiving funds from the United States. This meant that initial ideas for projects in the community, while positive and constructive, nonetheless needed to be framed in the correct way for us to be able to consider them for funding. As the grantmaker, it was critical that we assume the role of educator, working with our partners in BCause, the village leadership, and residents themselves to find ways to help everyone involved develop project ideas in full compliance with the applicable regulations.

Because the nonprofit community in Voditsa was not well established, this learning experience with BCause and the other stakeholders became instrumental to the successful implementation of the Rinker Ashley Fund's goals. Everyone's reputation (see the 3Rs) was on the line. We needed our partners in Bulgaria to understand our limitations as grantors, while we needed their help to identify needs in the community and organize tailored solutions to local problems. Although we did not necessarily need to work through an intermediary such as BCause to establish local oversight, ensure cultural sensitivity, remain in compliance, and to carry out needed due diligence, they were ultimately invaluable in this process.

Our experience in Voditsa is a good example of the importance of the 3Rs as a framework for international grantmaking, while also highlighting the importance of flexibility and the recruitment of well-vetted local implementing partners who helped create intercultural success in a remote international village.

Lessons Learned

In early 2017 I had the pleasure to visit Voditsa, five years after I first became involved in the project and six years since the beginning of the Fund's activities. Since then, together we have gone on to rebuild every major community building in the village,

educate scores of children, install a new water system (including replacing decades-old pipes from the era of communism in Bulgaria), and rebuild the clock tower in the town square that was damaged during an earthquake over thirty years ago.

My visit to the village in April 2017 coincided with the ribbon cutting ceremony for the refurbished village clock tower, which was repaired through a grant from the Rinker Ashley Fund after having been broken for decades.

Reflecting on the experience, trust between a grantmaker and grantee is very important when the grantee is operating in a foreign country, as cultural and regulatory barriers are not immediately obvious but should be anticipated. This can add to the complexity of effective communication—as we experienced in Voditsa, simple errors in context or translation can nearly derail an entire project. It is important to understand that nonprofits outside the United States may lack the technical knowledge to work directly with US grantmakers effectively. Flexibility within a strong due diligence protocol becomes an important aspect still to learn while placing emphasis on building the capacity of local implementing partners.

A Legal and Practical Guide

This book will provide you with the tools, knowledge, and information you need to manage an international grantmaking program effectively. With the 3Rs as your guide, each chapter of this book will highlight a different aspect of what will result in a successful international grantmaking strategy.

We will begin this book with an overview of international philanthropy, its history, and the ongoing conversations that are relevant to practitioners; here you will see many aspects of the Voditsa Bulgaria case study come to light. We will then take an in-depth look at how to ensure regulatory compliance with the IRS. Following this, we will look at what constitutes an effective and efficient due diligence process and how you can manage risks and protect reputations in a world plagued with concerns about terrorism and money laundering. Lastly, we will conclude this book with chapters that explore other practical considerations such as preparing for an audit, conducting monitoring and impact measurement, and considerations for wealth advisors and corporations.

Our goal for writing this book is for it to convey the most current information, best practices, and relevant case studies at its time of publishing.

We have designed this book to provide important information for both the novice and experienced international grantmaker.

Go change the world with your well designed, fully vetted, regulatory-compliant, risk-managed, reputation-enriching international philanthropy!

Ted Hart, ACFRE, CAP®

Ted Hart, ACFRE, CAP®, President and CEO, CAF America, brings over thirty years of experience in advising global philanthropy. As an internationally recognized speaker, Ted is an expert in both domestic and global philanthropic regulations and risk management. During his tenure as President and CEO, CAF America has witnessed exponential growth, significantly expanded its suite of services, and dramatically increased the number of charities funded around the world.

Before joining CAF America, Ted served as President of an international consultancy firm, providing strategic solutions to major nonprofits and NGOs. He has coauthored six books published by John Wiley & Sons, including *People to People Fundraising, Internet Management for Nonprofits,* and *Fundraising on the Internet.* Ted played a critical role in the creation of the green nonprofits movement and was founder of the international ePhilanthropy Foundation.

In addition to his Master in Public Administration (MPA) degree, Ted is a Chartered Advisor in Philanthropy (CAP), he holds the Advanced Certified Fundraising Executive (ACFRE) designation which is held globally by fewer than 120 people, and is certified in Anti-Money Laundering (AML/CFT) by the Society of Tax and Estate Professionals (STEP).

Chapter One

The Thriving Ecosystem of International Philanthropy

Adam Pickering

There can be few overviews of international philanthropy that do not attempt to place the issue within a dramatic narrative. As a student of global philanthropy and of history, and a reader of historical literature on the subject, you may feel that every successive year sees unprecedented challenges for or else a new high-water mark for global philanthropy. This chapter will be different in one respect; that I believe that both of these dramatic statements can be applied simultaneously. Furthermore, I believe that as readers of this book, you are a self-selecting audience of the people who are best placed to take advantage of the opportunities and respond to the challenges of our time.

Happily, the notion that international giving has never been healthier is eminently supportable with evidence. According to the 2017 *Giving USA Report*, private giving to "international affairs" is estimated to have reached $22.03 billion in 2016, an increase of 5.8 percent and a staggering 20.7 percent since 2014. This is in spite of a reduction in humanitarian appeal responses,[3] which might well have wiped out gains in years with less robust fundamental growth. Such growth is buttressed by the overall growth in American giving, which has grown in all nine of the categories measured by Giving USA for only the sixth time in forty years. However, international affairs is a cause that's first among equals, hav-

---

[3] Giving USA Foundation, Giving USA 2017: *The Annual Report on Philanthropy for the Year 2016* (Chicago: Giving USA Foundation, 2017), *givingusa.org/tag/giving-usa-2017*.

ing expanded to account for 6 percent of private philanthropy from 4 percent the previous year. Whether overall giving to international causes is a useful barometer for cross-border giving to foreign nonprofits is difficult to ascertain, but it is unlikely that there is no positive relationship between both forms of international funding.

Running parallel to this unquestionably positive narrative for cross-border giving are challenges which will test not only the mettle of US donors and the organizations which they support, they will question some of the most basic assumptions on which our giving is often based. In the coming years, we will have to deal with questions about legitimacy, transparency, power, and inequality. The world is becoming ever more interconnected and as a result, more complex. Ideas travel faster, groups coalesce quicker, and the sociopolitical climate can change in an instant. In an era of rapidly declining institutional trust, philanthropy is far from immune.[4] We will have to consider the universality of our rights as donors and the impact of our giving not only on beneficiaries but on ever-increasing circles of influence: communities, civil society, social attitudes, trust, and the economy as well.

Then there are the challenges of medium. While we are still coming to terms with existing ideas such as social investment or venture philanthropy, we will also be increasingly confronted by ever more disruptive innovations. New technologies will lead to bewildering options we haven't imagined yet. Would you like to release funds to charities when targets are met via a smart contract on the Blockchain? Would you like to be assisted in making more effective gifts by a powerful algorithm? Will these ideas have unintended negative consequences? Will they augment or replace tried and tested traditional approaches to philanthropy? Sometimes, the only way to assess the prognosis for the future is to look to the past.

A Brief History of US Philanthropy

It took a foreigner to sum up America's predilection for charitable enterprise when in 1835 Alexis de Tocqueville wrote that as "soon as several of the inhabitants of the United States have taken up an opinion or a feeling which they wish to promote to the world they look out for mutual

---

[4] "2017 Edelman Trust barometer," Edelman, accessed September 4, 2017 *edelman.com/trust2017.*

assistance."[5] However, strictly speaking, philanthropy of any formal or institutional nature was slow to get off the ground in what is now the United States. "Legislatures generally refused to grant equity jurisdiction to colonial courts, and without them, trusts—charitable and testamentary—were unenforceable, resulting in the misdirection or failure of early charitable trusts."[6] However, regardless of the legal environment, philanthropy and association were as entwined in the fabric of the United States as any other cultural fiber one could care to mention.

Notwithstanding the fact that many settlers from Europe thought of themselves as enlightened volunteers or that a culture of mutual association was vital to the survival of early pioneers to North America, charitable endeavor was highly regarded by a pious society committed to creating a more just world, free from the yolk of an overbearing state. Boston minister Cotton Mather (1663–1728), the first American to be elected to the Royal Society was heavily influenced by the thoughts of British Enlightenment scientists on the plight of the urban poor. He became an influential voice in "advocating 'friendly visiting' of the poor, the use of voluntary associations for mutual support, and philanthropic giving by the rich to relieve the poor and support schools, colleges, and hospitals."[7] As America industrialized and came to experience its own urban problems, Mather's words were to grow in importance.

But if early US philanthropic thought was influenced by European thinkers, it didn't take long for a distinctly US model of philanthropy to begin to influence European thinkers. US philanthropy has always been progressive and creative. Indeed, during the Victorian period, British commentators bemoaned the fact that their US cousins were more advanced, with the editor of *The Times* newspaper "inclined to credit American testators with greater liberality and more interesting ideas than their British counterparts. The bulk of British bequests, the editor insisted, came from childless persons, with no family responsibilities, and went for pretty conventional objects."[8]

_____

[5] Alexis de Tocqueville and Thomas Bender, *Democracy in America*. (New York: Modern Library, 1981).

[6] Peter Dobkin Hall, "A Historical Overview of Philanthropy, Voluntary Associations, and Nonprofit Organizations in the United States, 1600–2000," *In The Nonprofit Sector: A Research Handbook*, Second Edition. Richard Steinberg and Walter W. Powell (New Haven, CT: Yale University Press, 2006).

[7] Ibid.

[8] David Owen, *English Philanthropy, 1660-1960* (Cambridge, MA: Harvard University Press, 1964).

Cross-Border Giving by Americans

In this way, US philanthropy has always been an influencer of, and influenced by, international philanthropy. Philanthropists have always sought continuous improvement by sharing ideas across borders, and though US donors are preeminent regarding their generosity, to traverse an ever more difficult global landscape as donors they must listen and learn from local experts. That is a lesson more important now than ever because as donors, we not only represent causes, we also represent the idea of a pluralistic global civil society to cultures that, like the embryonic United States, must evolve existing cultures of generosity and association into forms which will be sustainable in the future.

It is easy to think of cross-border giving as something of a new phenomenon. However, the history of US philanthropy has never been isolationist in nature. Indeed, the existence of a tax deduction for charitable giving owes its existence to international affairs. Having been rejected in the original 1913 Revenue Act, the War Revenue Act 1917 allowed charitable deductions on the basis that they had proved to be a crucial part of the war effort. *The Washington Post* pointed out that, "If the money thus contributed were subject to taxes it would be a penalty upon generosity and an inducement for the retention by individuals of all moneys which they formerly contributed to charitable, scientific and educational institutions," and, inevitably, "the burden of maintaining such national auxiliaries as the Red Cross would fall entirely upon the Federal Government."[9] Indeed, geographical limitations on deductibility did not come into force until the 1938 Revenue Act and only after the 1935 Revenue Act had placed restrictions on corporate deductibility.

While the idea that the might of the US donor is a foreign policy asset which augments military might have seen its popularity wane, those in government have long understood that military power has its limitations and that "persuasion through soft power can yield more concession, cooperation, and enduring support [...] than coercion alone."[10] The unique nature of philanthropy is recognized as having particular relevance in this realm. Being a product of society, rather than government, bestows a sense of cultural freedom and unshackled human endeavor which often results in a less cynical response abroad, and hence enables

---

[9] "Charity Exempted," *Washington Post*, September 10, 1917.
[10] Joseph S. Nye, Jr., Soft Power: *The Means of Success in World Politics*. (New York: Public Affairs, 2004).

philanthropy and the organizations it supports to be more effective. Paradoxically, allowing independent altruism to leach through national borders has the effect of enhancing the national reputation and hence soft power.[11] At a time when diplomatic and aid budgets are being cut both by the United States and many of its foreign partners, this may well be a role that US donors see an increasing need to fill.

Trends in Giving

So if history teaches us that US donors always have and will continue to be interested in cross-border giving and that this giving has helped to export the virtues of a pluralistic international civil society, what does it teach us about how we should respond to new forms of giving?

Philanthropy has always changed to reflect new trends in the way resources are generated and today's generation is no different. The assumption that blending our for-profit and our not-for-profit endeavors together into *philanthrocapitalism*[12] is a new phenomenon is misguided. In his book on the history of British philanthropy, my colleague Rhodri Davies dispels any notion that this trend is somehow a recent innovation with aplomb by detailing numerous historical examples of such practices. As Davies puts it, if anything, the *discovery* that commercial and philanthropic approaches can be blended is more of a rediscovery of something our forebears took for granted.[13]

One such example is that of Thomas Firmin who employed 1,600 spinners as weavers under a loss-making enterprise with the sole purpose of employing poor people in the community, and "Firmin conceived of his enterprise as thrifty philanthropy rather than as an ordinary business."[14] He was clear that "he could look upon a loss of twopence in the shilling as money well spent"[15] and contributed an annual investment of between £2,000 and £4,000 to the businesses.

---

[11] Helmut K. Anheier and Adele Simmons, "The Role of Philanthropy in Globalization," in: *Rethinking Philanthropic Effectiveness: Lessons from an International Network of Foundation Experts*. Dirk Eilinghoff (Gütersloh: Bertelsmann Stiftung, 2005).
[12] Michael Edwards, "Gates, Google, and the Ending of Global Poverty: Philanthrocapitalism and International Development" *The Brown Journal of World Affairs* 15(2), 35-42 (2009).
[13] Rhodri Davies, *Public Good by Private Means: How Philanthropy Shapes Britain* (London: Charities Aid Foundation and Alliance Publishing Trust, 2015).
[14] Owen, 1964.
[15] Ibid.

So if blurring the boundaries of business and philanthropy isn't new what has changed to make this idea seem particularly interesting to so many people? Part of the answer is that the nature of business ownership has changed. Increasingly, businesses are owned by shareholders or investment companies, and their global profile often makes mobilizing the kind of philanthropic resources seen by corporate foundations much more difficult. However, in this climate, more and more philanthropically minded entrepreneurs are looking to lock such philanthropic missions into the heart of their companies through new organizational forms such as B-Corporations or through social investment models. That, of course, should be welcomed, but it also invites (even philosophical) questions about the role of philanthropy.

There is a danger that the kind of giving that many of us engage in is going to be soon seen as outdated. Simply giving money to an organization predominantly funded by donations may seem unsophisticated in a world of new and exciting blended approaches. However, I believe, and the longevity of traditional forms of philanthropy certainly attests, that such simple donations—with the appropriate validation and evaluation—will not only continue to have an important role in society but will always be one of the most powerful tools for change available.

This is because while market-based approaches to improving the world can do a huge amount of good—without question, the for-profit world could contribute orders of magnitude more money to the $1.4 trillion it is estimated would be needed to deliver the Sustainable Development Goals (SDGs) for example—there are things which exist outside the market. For example, some people on this planet are so poor or so isolated as to have no route into the financial system and helping them will present few opportunities for profit. Equally, those who seek not to correct market failures but to change the social contract, to transform the socioeconomic system, or to challenge tradition will struggle to find a profitable way of doing so. While it is true that companies often drive social progression—witness the recent examples of companies supporting same sex marriage or pledging to deliver on environmental promises following the United States exit from the Paris Climate Agreement—this only happens when a cause reaches a threshold of public acceptance. Few companies are openly campaigning in Uganda for LGBTQ rights; thanks to foreign donors, civil society organizations are.

We have established that the history of cross-border giving in the United States is long and illustrious but we must also recognize that international philanthropy really took off in the mid to late 20th Century. The civil rights movement became globally focused and played a role in countering apartheid in South Africa. Later on, donors aided the transition to democracy of nations after the fall of the Berlin Wall. The 1980s saw an awakening of mass popular engagement in humanitarian relief through events such as Band Aid. Cross-border giving was experiencing unprecedented growth and the nonprofit organizations it supported were flowering into civil society movements around the world.

Threats to Civil Society Across the Globe

However, after a period of unchecked growth, cross-border giving would reach an inflection point at the dawn of the millennium as challenges began to emerge to the philanthropic freedoms enjoyed by donors and the operating environment for the organizations they fund.

For Doug Rutzen, Director of the International Center for Not-for-profit Law (ICNL) the crucial turning point was the attacks on the World Trade Center on September 11, 2001. Civil society organizations found themselves under scrutiny as potential vehicles for the financing of terror while also becoming co-opted into the war effort as part of the post-conflict democratization project. This, according to Rutzen has led to a more cynical appraisal of international civil society that characterizes nonprofits, and by extension, philanthropy, as a Trojan Horse for regime change.

> On the one hand, the sector was targeted under the War on Terror. On the other, the Bush Administration embedded support for civil society into the Freedom Agenda. For both reasons—the association of civil society with terrorism and the association of civil society with Bush's Freedom Agenda—governments around the world became increasingly concerned about civil society, particularly CSOs that received international support.

—Doug Rutzen, Director, International Center for Not-for-profit Law.[16]

The foreign aid, technical assistance, and diplomatic funding provided by the United States has often sought the same goals as US donors—advancing democracy, enhancing the rule of law, and promoting human

---

[16] Douglas Rutzen, "Aid Barriers and the Rise of Philanthropic Protectionism" *International Journal of Not-for-Profit Law* vol. 17, No. 1 (2015).

rights. When foreign governments began to see the foreign funding of civil society movements encroach on their sphere of influence, they cried foul without making a distinction between private philanthropy and state funding. One of the first leaders to articulate a counternarrative which depicts the foreign funding of civil society as antidemocratic foreign meddling was Vladimir Putin.

President Putin and pro-Russian Ukrainians suspected that the protests in Kiev were being orchestrated by foreign, namely US forces, through puppet nonprofits. For those who grew up under the Iron Curtain and the climate of suspicion and paranoia that is synonymous with society in a police state, this must have seemed entirely plausible. Putin accused the United States of pursuing a "dictatorial" foreign policy, packaged in "beautiful, pseudodemocratic phraseology" and he succeeded to some extent in undermining the credibility of nonprofits receiving funding from the US.[17] This was the fracture which started an avalanche of regimes which were nervous of being accountable to the increasing power of a growing global philanthropy.

According to data from ICNL, between 2004 and 2010, more than fifty countries considered or enacted measures restricting civil society.[18] In 2010 the trend shifted to the Arab world in earnest as governments—in a mirroring of what happened after Ukraine's Orange Revolution—reacted by constricting the freedoms of association and assembly and undermining connections with foreign funders in response to the Arab Spring. The trend—by then referred to as the *closing* or *shrinking space for civil society*—accelerated and globalized between 2012 and 2015 with "more than ninety laws constraining the freedoms of association or assembly [having] been proposed or enacted." It has only slowed of late because there is now so little space left for further constriction.

While it is part of a wider closing space for civil society, the recent trend for governments to impose barriers on foreign donors is a trend in and of itself, and different governments are employing different strategies for limiting the flow of foreign donations. I see the most important typologies of approaches that create barriers to US cross-border grantmaking as follows:

---

[17] William Schneider, "Ukraine's 'Orange Revolution.'" Atlantic, December 2004 Issue, accessed 12 July 2017.
theatlantic.com/magazine/archive/2004/12/ukraines-orange-revolution/305157.
[18] Rutzen, 2015.

Populist, Nationalist Isolationism

For example, many countries follow what might be termed as a populist, nationalist approach which typecasts organizations that receive foreign funding as traitorous. Such an approach usually means creating vague laws on the foreign funding of *political activities*. This is the case of Russia where the 2012 Foreign Agents Law requires any nonprofit receiving foreign funds that engages in "political activities" to register as a "foreign agent" and a 2015 law on *undesirable organizations* creates a blacklist of foreign organizations which hands the state extrajudicial powers to close them down. Such vagueness creates uncertainty that may result in conservatism in the sector, which breeds fear and suspicion and results in self-policing and the refusal of foreign gifts. In addition, state-controlled media and government rhetoric may be utilized to undermine trust in the international donor community. This populist strategy for restricting foreign donor access could be said to be in use in Venezuela, Bolivia, and former Soviet nations such as Belarus and Hungary, where the Prime Minister Viktor Orbán has stated, "We are not dealing with civil society activists but with paid political activists who are trying to help foreign interests."[19]

Such rhetoric appears to be increasing and is even reaching nations that are underpinned by entrenched cultures and laws supporting civic freedoms. For example, in South Africa Minister of State Security, David Mahlobo stated in 2016 that "[t]here are certain NGOs in SA, you know them and I know them too. There are questions of who funds them and why their funders [are] doing certain things […] Let's not hide it, these are [the] geopolitics of the world. Because of geopolitics, certain NGOs are planted here to work as a front."[20]

Restrictions on the Grounds of Security Concerns

Ever since the 9/11 terrorist attacks, the global effort to stem the flow of terrorist finances has had unintended negative consequences for donors wishing to get money to nonprofits operating in some of the world's most dangerous, and therefore, in need places. The increased

---

[19] Lydia Gall, "Dispatches: The End of Liberal Democracy in Hungary?" *Human Rights Watch*, 2014, accessed July 13, 2017,
hrw.org/news/2014/07/29/dispatches-end-liberal-democracy-hungary.
[20] "Lack of state accountability raises concerns over surveillance in South Africa."
The Daily Vox, 2017, accessed 13 July 2017,
thedailyvox.co.za/lack-state-accountability-raises-concerns-surveillance-south-africa.

remit and influence of the Financial Action Taskforce (FATF) meant that its assertion that nonprofit organizations "are particularly vulnerable, and countries should ensure that they cannot be misused"[21] caused governments and regulators to increase their scrutiny, and huge fines in the courts for banks found guilty of abetting money laundering have led to increasing compliance costs, an ever-reducing risk appetite, and ultimately a reduction in the flow of resources to some parts of the world. That FATF has recently—thanks to a prolonged campaign by global civil society—changed this definition to a more proportionate statement is to be lauded.[22] However, it has not curtailed the ever-tightening net of compliance constraints and bank de-risking activities in many parts of the world. While in many countries this is simply a regrettable side effect of the quite understandable desire to combat terrorist financing, some governments have used FATF as a pretext for restricting foreign donor access with the 2010 Foreign Contribution Regulation Act in India and the 2009 NGO Policy in Sierra Leone being recent examples.[23]

More widely, policies that piggyback on the security agenda to restrict foreign funding to nonprofits are rife. As Green and Baydas summarize, "Algeria, Bangladesh, Russia, Tunisia, and Venezuela, for example, issued regulations that mandate additional scrutiny of financial institutions' transactions and cap foreign funding for organizations engaged in human rights and advocacy efforts."[24] One strategy that is used to discourage foreign donors is imposing excessive bureaucratic requirements such as requiring prior approval to be a recipient of foreign funds (Pakistan, Sri Lanka and China) and even for every individual cross-border gift (Jordan, Algeria, Belarus).

[21] Financial Action Task Force, *International Standards on Combating Money Laundering and the Financing of Terrorism and Proliferation: The FATF Recommendations* (Paris: FATF/OECD, 2012).
[22] Countries should review the adequacy of laws and regulations that relate to nonprofit organizations which the country has identified as being vulnerable to terrorist financing abuse. *International Standards on Combating Money Laundering and the Financing of Terrorism and Proliferation: The FATF Recommendations* (Paris: FATF/ OECD, February 2012) Updated October 2016. p. 13.
[23] Iva Dobichina and Poonam Joshi, "In the name of security: when silencing active citizens creates even greater problems," *Open Democracy*, accessed July 13, 2017. *opendemocracy.net*.
[24] Shannon N. Green and Lana Baydas, "Counterterrorism Measures: Pretext for Closing the Space for Civil Society," *Center for Strategic and International Studies*, 2017, accessed July 13, 2017, *csis.org*.

Appropriation of the Effectiveness Agenda

That we, philanthropy, should seek to be ever more effective and that transparency and openness is an important part of that effort is far from controversial. However, perhaps because both donors and nonprofits have recognized the need for greater transparency and accountability for international funding, some governments have been able to subtly employ this language in creating systems that skew global philanthropy in their own favor.

David Donahue, Irish UN representative and cofacilitator of the SDGs, made it clear at an event I attended in 2015 that freedom of expression had been downplayed and human rights practically excluded in the closed-door negations on the seventeen goals and 169 targets laid out in the SDG agenda. To be clear, I believe that philanthropy should be—as it has been encouraged to be in the United Nation's own financing plans[25]—encouraged to play as big a role as possible in delivering on what is an extraordinary agreement to make our world a better and fairer place. However, as nations pull together their national action plans for delivering on selected targets, some will use that process to attempt to pull in global philanthropy that supports their agenda and suppress that which does not. Calling for transparency could become a government tool for exposing such funds and the term *effective* could be used to mean *compliant*.

Indeed, there is evidence that this warping of the effectiveness agenda is already occurring. For example, India has stated on behalf of the Like Minded Group of Countries—a group of countries which often vote together at the United Nations[26]—that "advocacy for civil society should be tempered by the need for responsibility, openness and transparency and accountability of civil society organizations."[27] That statement looks more targeted when one considers that India has subsequently settled on a much tougher interpretation of its 2010 Foreign Contribution Regulation Act (FCRA), which has seen numerous organizations have

---

[25] United Nations, *World Investment Report 2014, Investing in the SDGs: An Action Plan*, The United Nations Conference on Trade and Development, 2014.
[26] The Like Minded Group of Developing Countries (LMDC) includes: Algeria, Bangladesh, Belarus, Bhutan, China, Cuba, Egypt, India, Indonesia, Iran, Malaysia, Myanmar, Nepal, Pakistan, The Philippines, Sri Lanka, Sudan, Syria, Vietnam, and Zimbabwe.
[27] "25th Session Joint Statement: Panel discussion on the importance of the promotion and protection of civil society space," Human Rights Council, 2014.

their licenses to receive foreign funds revoked. As such, it may be that as funding inevitably gravitates toward SDG targets, it does so at the expense of those causes which have been left out. In this climate, brave and controversial philanthropy may become increasingly rare and increasingly precious.

This emerging global landscape is one that poses considerable challenges for US cross-border donors. On the one hand, the need to support civil society abroad in countries where they are coming under pressure from government has never been greater. On the other hand, there is a real danger that funding under these circumstances could make the situation worse by either seeming to vindicate the accusation of excessive and illegal foreign meddling or by placing those who receive money in danger. As such, some donors may cease to make cross-border gifts out of fear of causing harm. It is crucial that they do not. Rather, we need to seek professional advice in making cross-border donations or to educate ourselves and the organizations to which we donate. The increasing prevalence of cause or geographical focused *giving circles*, where donors engage in peer learning, appears to be an organic and welcome response to this need.

In the course of this chapter, we have covered some of the principal challenges to contemporary international grantmakers. However, we should not allow ourselves to disregard the huge potential for global philanthropy in the coming years. Indeed, possibly the most striking long-term trend in Charities Aid Foundation's World Giving Index has been the steady rise in giving in transitional economies—countries that are experiencing rapid development but are not yet wealthy. Though those living in transitioning economies remain less likely to donate money every month (20 percent) than those living in the developing world (26 percent), an increase of 2.1 percentage points in 2016 on the back of an increase of 11.5 percentage points in 2015 suggests that the gap is narrowing.[28] This signals the huge potential—one which CAF has highlighted as part of its Groundwork for Growing Giving campaign—for the emerging middle classes in transitional economies to support philanthropic activity in the world's fast-growing economies. The campaign calculates that were the 2.4 billion people who are projected to enter the middle classes worldwide by 2030 to give just 0.5 percent of their spend-

---

[28] Charities Aid Foundation, *World Giving Index 2016*, Charities Aid Foundation, 2016. Accessed July 14, 2017, *cafonline.org*.

ing over to charitable causes, it could amount to $319 billion annually for good causes.[29]

This potential for the growth of philanthropy in other countries is by no means tangential to US grantmaking. Building sustainable civil societies that can win public trust and support means providing resources to local organizations that are initiated and controlled by local communities. However, the global funding landscape often rewards large international nonprofits above locally trusted ones. While large western headquartered organizations are doing important work, the fact that in 2011 it was estimated that only 1 percent of global official development assistance from governments was granted directly to Southern-based nonprofits suggests that more needs to be done to balance the market. This is why cross-border grantmaking from private citizens is becoming ever more important. Increasingly, the generosity of US grantmakers is helping to create an environment that encourages more and more of the world's emerging middle classes to engage in philanthropy: "We have moved to an era in which global partnerships are most effective when they create an environment that allows the general public to contribute to solving problems. The partnerships that inspire movements of hundreds of thousands of people advocating, educating, and fundraising for one end goal are the new recipe for sustainable solutions."[30]

As we face new opportunities and challenges, American grantmakers will need to be ever more adaptable to the changing context, but at the same time, it is crucial that they retain the key features highlighted in this chapter, which has allowed them to play such an important role in the world to date.

---

[29] Adam Pickering, *Laying the Groundwork for Growing Giving: A 2017 update to Unlocking the Potential of Global Philanthropy*, Charities Aid Foundation, 2017.
[30] Elizabeth Gore and Kent Ford, "Joe Public: The Most Important Partner in International Philanthropy," *Georgetown Journal of International Affairs* Summer/Fall 2012, pp. 31-37.

Adam Pickering

After more than a decade working in policy and thought leader-ship roles in civil society, Adam now serves as a Policy Advisor on civil society to the British government within the Department for International Development (DFID).

Before working for DFID, Adam spent five years at Charities Aid Foundation (CAF) where he led on international policy, contributed publications, and spoke on a wide range of issues as part of CAF's in-house think tank, Giving Thought.

An expert on civil society, international development, accountabil-ity, and international nonprofit law, Adam has also worked for the National Council for Voluntary Organisations (NCVO) and the Centre for Public Scrutiny among other organizations in the UK and India.

Chapter Two

Unite and Conquer: Giving in the Context of the Sustainable Development Goals

Heather Grady

Forged over three years of negotiations and formally signed by all governments in September 2015, the seventeen Sustainable Development Goals (SDGs) are no less than a road map for the world's future. They replaced the Millennium Development Goals (MDGs), which to a great extent guided official development assistance and other aid programs in the 2001-2015 period.

The process of both the MDGs and the SDGs was stewarded by the United Nations (UN), but the MDGs were largely an *insiders'* game where the UN and governments debated and then aimed to reach their targets. The SDGs arose out of the understanding that the field of international assistance and development needed to embrace a much more ambitious and comprehensive starting point and endpoint. Moreover, the SDGs were taken up by civil society actors at the early negotiation stage unlike the MDGs, which were largely crafted inside the halls of the UN. A full list of the seventeen goals and 169 targets can be found here.[31]

The SDGs have similarities to the MDGs: for example, the time period for achievement is the same (only half a generation), each goal has associated targets, and there is overlap in some of the broad areas like poverty, gender equality, and health. But they are fundamentally different in many ways. First, they are considered highly interdependent and

---

[31] "Sustainable Development Goals," United Nations, accessed July 22, 2017. *un.org/sustainabledevelopment/sustainable-development-goals*.

interrelated, and they weave together causes and solutions for social, economic and environmental problems. Inequality rose from obscurity to its own goal. Inclusive societies, accountable governance, and peace feature prominently (a move objected to in the negotiations by many governments). Crucially they are *universal* just as the international human rights framework is universal; they are absolute and cover every-one and everywhere, applying to countries rich and poor. This is part of what makes them so compelling; the world had not previously had a normative framework that acknowledged poverty in the midst of plenty, which is a reality that is becoming all too common.

But unlike the architecture of human rights laws and treaties, the SDGs are not binding on governments, and so it becomes exceedingly impor-tant that so-called non-state actors—all of the institutions across civil society, philanthropy, business, media, and academia—hold govern-ments to account for the commitments they have made. In the view of some, this may be a more effective strategy for accountability since it relies on ongoing public pressure and campaign-like tactics rather than justiciability in courts, which has had its limits in effectively forcing governments and businesses to follow the rules.

Goal thirteen addresses climate change on both the mitigation side, reducing human actions that contribute to greenhouse gas emissions, and on the adaptation side, supporting people to cope with and become resilient to the inevitable effects of climate change. So the responsibility for action which previously only sat with the UN Framework Convention on Climate Change (UNFCCC) is now spread more widely across a variety of UN agencies, government departments, and those outside in business, civil society, and philanthropy. Like the comparison with human rights negotiations, it lifts the locus of action more into the pub-lic domain and allows a broader range of actors to have voice and agency in compelling those with responsibility and power to act.

The SDGs were also additive to the Human Development Index, which is a highly useful tool to compare specific indicators across countries.

What Role Can Philanthropy Play in this Framework?

During the period of the MDGs, the philanthropy sector overall had a very limited input into, or even knowledge of, the processes and potential of the goals. The MDGs were seen as the domain of donor, the recipient governments, and the UN. Many in the philanthropy sector have kept a distance from working with governments, sometimes bearing an antipathy to working with partners who were seen as bureaucratic, lethargic, or even authoritarian. There were notable exceptions, particularly in the field of health, where usually the larger foundations and philanthropists made grants or formed alliances that provided benefits to, and benefited from, global goals driving diverse resource pools toward shared outcomes.

In the SDGs period, the situation is significantly different. A far greater range of philanthropic actors are either experimenting with or wholeheartedly embracing the SDGs as a way to scale their impact and leverage their resources with those of like-minded partners. The section below examines both the challenges and the potential.

The Challenges of Engaging with the SDGs

The challenges, indeed, are not to be dismissed. The philanthropy sector—made up of foundations, individual philanthropists, divisions of companies, crowd-funding mechanisms, and other actors who voluntarily provide private resources for public benefit—tends to see itself as firmly and proudly independent and autonomous. Freed from the constraints of government budget prioritizing, or a focus on narrow financial returns, those in the philanthropy sector have far fewer incentives than business or nonprofits to act collectively for efficiency or effectiveness. While adapting their giving to public agendas or targets may scale and leverage their impact, there are unique qualities of philanthropy sector institutions that may limit this approach. There are at least three reasons. First, they define their own priorities generally according to their founder's and/or current board of directors' values, wishes, and passions—generally not according to a calculus of what most needs to be done, where existing gaps are, or what would be the most cost-efficient intervention. Second, the predominant form of group organizational structure is generally membership organizations or affinity groups (based on theme or location) that have few if any incentives, let alone norms, for coordinating their giving. Third, there is no external accountability framework beyond following the law—stakeholders outside are generally reluctant to pressure those who give them grants to be more effective because it is *biting the hand that feeds you*, so feedback is rare and often anonymized through standardized surveys that may not ask anything about the foregone benefits of joining public agendas for scaling impact.

Why Should Philanthropy Engage with the SDGs?

Yet the advantages of being more responsive to adapting to, or even adopting, society's shared frameworks and public agendas, like the SDGs, are many. There has been interest in the last decade in the notion of *collective impact* in the philanthropy sector, and a slow but steady increase in donor collaboratives around systems change—like climate change funder networks—indicate that the SDGs are coming at a time when funders realize that working together will take them farther, if not faster, toward sustainable impact.

In a recent article for the European Research Network on Philanthropy's 8th International Conference, we suggested a set of six strategies that support greater impact and reaching scale:[32]

◆ Becoming aware of trends and intersections and building on them;

◆ Tapping networks for extended influence;

◆ Understanding how collecting and sharing data can enable funders to be more collaborative and effective;

◆ Collaborating with governments;

◆ Developing pathways to scale solutions; and

◆ Driving innovation.

Interestingly and perhaps not surprisingly, the subset of philanthropy whose uptake on the SDGs is fastest is impact investors, exemplified by several networks adopting the SDGs as a logical shared investment and measurement framework. Notable examples include the Global Impact Investing Network, Confluence Philanthropy, TONIIC, and several European responsible investing institutions that hold funds for high net worth individuals. This reflects the economic efficiencies sought by those who are investment minded as well as the comfort—and even imperative—that impact investors have in seeking deal partners.

This is very different from the *go it alone* approaches more common in philanthropy. But we know philanthropy will be engaged implicitly if not explicitly: Brad Smith of the Foundation Center estimates that phi-

---

[32] Callias et al, "Philanthropy's Contributions to the Sustainable Development Goals in Emerging Countries," European Research Network on Philanthropy 8th International Conference, 2017.

lanthropy will contribute a minimum of US $364 billion to the SDGs before 2030 on current trends.[33]

Platforms and networks around the SDGs found success in the last few years in a way they likely would not have in the 2000-2015 period. One example is the SDG Philanthropy Platform (*SDGphilanthropy.org*) whose underlying philosophy is that bringing philanthropy to the table where government, the UN system, civil society, and business are already planning and implementing will bring faster progress toward achieving the SDGs as well as enhance the impact and effectiveness (or efficiency) of each funder's giving. This seems to demonstrate results fastest at the country level where stakeholders develop an ongoing relationship and build trust to share more deeply.

The number of multi-sectoral partnerships around the SDGs is expand-ing. In the United States, the Council on Foundations is working with partners in several cities and regions as member foundations apply the SDGs as a framework to coordinate efforts around shared aims.[34] The Conrad N. Hilton Foundation has embraced the SDGs as a guide for many of its partnerships and achievements, and indeed points to their long-term partners the Catholic Sisters as the SDGs *personified*.[35] The Rockefeller Foundation launched a Zero Gap Initiative that employs a venture philanthropy model to support early-stage research and design and leans heavily on collaboration and experimentation with both pri-vate and public sector partners.[36] A new philanthropy coalition that aims to end violence against children is exploring how to find intersections with national and local SDG planning in South Africa and Tanzania.

In Africa, Asia, and the Middle East, funders are collaborating with the public sector and others in business and civil society around the goals. For example, in Ghana, the SDG Philanthropy Platform has formed an Advisory Group on SDG collaboration drawing from all sectors and is actively connecting foundations with Ministries of Finance, Water

---

[33] Brad Smith, "Foundations Will Contribute $364 Billion to SDGs," SDG *Philanthropy Platform*, accessed July 23, 2017, *sdgfunders.org/blog/foundations-will-contribute-364-billion-to-sdgs*.

[34] Alex Edwards, Berlin Rosen and Natalie Ross, *From Global Goals to Local Impact: How Philanthropy Can Help Achieve the U.N. Sustainable Development Goals in the U.S.*, Council on Foundations, 2016, *cof.org*.

[35] Tenille Metti, "Catholic Sisters: The Sustainable Development Goals Personified," *The Hilton Foundation*, accessed July 31, 2017, *hiltonfoundation.org/news/169-catholic-sisters-the-sustainable-development-goals-personified*.

[36] The Rockefeller Foundation, accessed July 23, 2017, *rockefellerfoundation.org*.

Resources, Education, and local government. It is positioning philan-thropy to work with the government on a more lasting basis to design effective strategies to achieve the SDGs. Using an approach typical in the philanthropy sector, SDG Philanthropy Platform staff in Ghana brought in a specialist in user-centered design to work on collaborative path-ways for the water sector to overcome seemingly intractable problems in designing sustainable systems and approaches.

A growing number of corporate foundations are engaging in the SDGs. The Impact 2030 initiative, for example, is a collaboration between the UN, social and public sectors, and academia, with the unique mission to activate human capital investments through employee volunteer pro-grams to advance the achievement of the SDGs.[37] Their approach is to activate, collaborate, and measure the impact of employee volunteer-ing on the SDGs. Companies from Blackbaud to Medtronic are bringing knowledge of the SDGs to their staff and corporate partners. The Business & Sustainable Development Commission encourages business leaders to seize upon sustainable development as an economic opportunity of a lifetime, and their flagship report, *Better Business, Better World*, illus-trates the benefits of not only corporate philanthropy but also wider company behavior aligning with the SDGs.[38]

Measuring impact is another potential advantage for philanthropy of adopting the SDG framework. After all, many of the world's best minds and most experienced practitioners negotiated and designed the sev-enteen goals and 169 targets. Many funders expend time and effort deciding how they will measure the impact of their funding. Aligning with targets that are not only proven to matter but against which a whole range of other actors will be collecting and reporting data, could reduce the expense and effort of any individual funder.

Linked to impact, the recent trend in philanthropy is to empha-size the importance of long-term systems change, going far beyond the approach of making discrete individual grants whose long-term impacts are not linked together in any significant way. The dominant discourse around this is betting on winning social entrepreneurs or sys-tem entrepreneurs by funding them over an appropriately long period of time and enabling them to build in innovation and risk-taking so that

---

[37] Impact2030, accessed July 28, 2017, *impact2030.com*.
[38] Business & Sustainable Development Commission (BSDC), accessed July 28, 2017, *businesscommission.org*.

they can adapt strategy as they learn, grow, and respond to changes in the external environment. While this is indeed a key step forward for funders who aim for sustained, systemic change, the impact would be greater still if that funding was set in the context of public agendas and agreed frameworks like the SDGs that allow any individual organization's work to find resonance among allies in the government, the UN system, and elsewhere.

Finally, the SDGs provide an opening for philanthropy to continue to work on creating an enabling environment in countries around the world for not only philanthropy but also broader civil society. The space for voluntary action and private initiative, especially if part of its intent is to hold government to account for its responsibilities, is under attack in many countries. This space must be preserved. The shared goals and government commitments of the SDGs provide an opportunity for a constructive dialogue to expand that space.

Heather Grady

Heather Grady is a Vice President at Rockefeller Philanthropy Advisors and leads strategy and program development in global philanthropy. She leads the SDG Philanthropy Platform to encourage philanthropy to engage more meaningfully in the Sustainable Development Goals, and the Scalable Solutions initiative, which supports funders to work collaboratively to place longer-term, adaptive resources to accelerate scalable solutions that target systemic changes. Heather serves as an Adjunct Professor at the China Global Philanthropy Institute.

Heather's philanthropic advising has been shaped in part by two decades living in countries in Asia, Africa, and the Middle East, managing development and humanitarian programs focused on a range of themes including education, livelihoods, health, agriculture, and microfinance. Heather was a Vice President at The Rockefeller Foundation where she managed a budget averaging $65 million. She served as Managing Director of Realizing Rights: The Ethical Globalization Initiative and was an Adjunct Professor at Columbia University.

Heather has degrees from Harvard University and Smith College. She serves on a number of boards and advisory groups including The B Team, the Business and Human Rights Resource Center, and the Wildlife Justice Commission. She is a member of the World Economic Forum Global Future Councils and the NationSwell Council.

Chapter Three

Ethics in International Grantmaking

Patricia Rosenfield

> *In philanthropy and civil society... foundations often hide behind the particulars of our missions, rather than standing up for the deeper values our missions embody... The challenges we face are global—and so is our crisis of leadership.*

—Darren Walker, President, Ford Foundation, *My Annual Letter: A call for moral courage in America,* September 6, 2017, *fordfoundation.org*

Philanthropy, unlike many other fields, does not have a code of ethics. Darren Walker's statement underscores that gap. My aim in this chapter is to provide guidance for you as an international grantmaker to help fill that gap by exercising ethical leadership.

Ethical grantmaking hinges on your having a clear understanding of the values, norms, and risks associated with the proposed activity. By asking a series of questions that will enable you to clarify these issues, you will enhance the sustainability—and thus the success—of your international programs or supported projects.

Basic Terms of Ethical International Grantmaking

It is not necessary to become an ethicist to engage in ethical grantmaking. At the same time, you might find it to be helpful to refresh your understanding of ethics before you discuss the subject with your colleagues and your grantees.[39]

Ethical frameworks build on moral principles, values, and standards to help guide both individual behaviors and social actions. The ethical deliberations in American society around social justice, healthcare, even local garbage collection, are based on such moral understanding.[40] A good example informs the core of ethical behavior in many fields, the medical Hippocratic Oath, "First, do no harm."

While it will be useful to understand a wide range of ethical traditions, for your practice I want to underline what two fellow international grantmakers and I wrote in 2004, "Ethical conduct in international grantmaking… requires… explicit attention to the wide range of questions that need to be asked to ensure public trust is fully sustained."[41] The framework presented later in this chapter provides you with a range of questions that will assist you in this regard. It is entirely likely that you will be able to add your own set of questions.

I am sure you are familiar with the following fundamental values that underpin all grantmaking. They also inform the ethical considerations discussed later:[42]

◆ Accountability—compliance with IRS regulations and pertinent foreign laws and regulations, as well as with your organization's and grantee's board, mission and public's expectations

◆ Transparency—providing the public and grantseeking communities with an honest, detailed rationale for the activity, grantee selection process, monitoring and evaluation procedures, exit strategies, and outreach and dissemination efforts

---

[39] Useful readings for me include: Jeffrey Olen, Julie C. Van Camp, and Vincent Barry, *Apply Ethics: A Text with Readings, Eighth Edition* (Belmont, CA: Wadsworth/Thomson Learning, 2005); William Damon and Susan Verducci, eds., *Taking Philanthropy Seriously: Beyond Noble Intentions to Responsible Grantmaking* (Bloomington, IN: Indiana University Press, 2006); Patricia Illingworth, Thomas Pogge, and Leif Wenar, eds., *Giving Well: The Ethics of International Philanthropy* (New York: Oxford University Press, 2011).
[40] Olen et al, *Applying Ethics*, 7.
[41] Patricia L. Rosenfield, Courtenay Sprague, and Heather McKay, "Ethical Dimensions of International Grantmaking: Drawing the Line in a Borderless World," *The Journal of Leadership and Organizational Studies*, 11, no. 1, (2004): 50-51.
[42] For a different view, see John Tyler, *Transparency in Philanthropy: An Analysis of Accountability, Fallacy, and Volunteerism* (Washington, D.C.: The Philanthropy Roundtable, 2013).

◆ Pluralism—listening to and respecting multiple perspectives about the activity—ensuring that, both within your organization and with grantees, differences across age, gender, and ethnicity, as well as methods and approaches, are well represented

◆ Collaboration—not working alone but discussing and working with other grantmakers and grantees based on shared values and trust[43]

Three additional terms inform ethical grantmaking in the twenty-first century: public trust, globalization, and partnership. The definitions I'm suggesting below broaden the scope of these terms. By considering them explicitly, you will enhance the likelihood that your efforts are ethically effective and sustainable.

Attributes of an Ethical International Grantmaker

Andrea Johnson, program officer, Carnegie Corporation of New York's Program on Higher Education and Research in Africa and Peacebuilding in Africa, recently discussed her approach to ethical international grantmaking (interview, September 10, 2017): "We [grantor and grantee] are all on the same side. That doesn't mean we are not held accountable for our work, because, in fact, grantees and foundations are not perfect, but we should all be aiming for the same goals."

Moreover, Johnson notes that as part of their efforts to strengthen research capacity, she and her colleagues also respect the knowledge of their partners. Grantees set their own agendas for research, network building, and institutional capacity strengthening. The point of reference is the grantees' own societies. This approach leads to quality results, with grantee efforts contributing to solving local and national problems.

Public Trust

US nonprofits are established as public trust institutions with state or national charters; tax exemption reinforces a nonprofit's obligation to work for the public good.[44] When US nonprofits, namely, those that are

---

[43] For an insightful discussion of this aspect, see, James Allen Smith, "In Search of an Ethic of Giving," in Damon and Verducci, *Taking Philanthropy Seriously*, 13-36, especially, 22-24.
[44] For two different analyses, see: Rob Reich, "Philanthropy and Caring for the Needs of Strangers," in Mack, *Giving*, 517-538.; Carl J. Schramm, "Law Outside the Market: The Social Utility of the Private Foundation, Harvard Journal of Law and Public Policy 30, No. 1 (Fall 2006): 356–407.

grantmaking organizations, work overseas, another aspect of public trust comes into play: the redefinition of *public*.

This leads to complex questions. Which public benefits from this project or program? The American public, whose taxes are foregone by the tax exemption but who may also benefit from the grants made in another country? Alternatively, is it the public in the nation where the project is based who directly benefits from that investment?

I contend that, foremost, it is the public where the project is based. Nonetheless, an often-neglected concern is, how would the American *public trust* benefit by your support of this international activity? What knowledge gained from this project is useful to the people in the United States? Discussing distinctive aspects of foreign and domestic public trust with potential local and international partners, including grantees, could lead to changes in the project design that make it both more ethical and more effective.

Globalization

Two distinguished American international relations scholars, Robert Keohane and Joseph Nye in 2000 wrote about four types of globalism that would contribute to the complexity of the twenty-first century: economic, military, environmental, and social and cultural.[45] These have all been well-recognized since then.

One globalism type, however, that they did not include has changed the nature of international grantmaking: the spread of grantmaking organizations throughout Europe, Asia, the Middle East, Africa, and Latin America.[46] It is now possible, in most settings, to redefine the role of the US international grantmaker in relation to their local grantees, as discussed below and indicated in the framework. This change also facilitates outside grantmakers responding to the public trust concerns.

---

[45] Robert O. Keohane and Joseph S. Nye, Jr, "Globalization: What's New? What's Not? (And so What?)," *Foreign Policy* 118 (Spring, 2000), 106-107.

[46] Examples of national, regional and global networks of local grantmaking organizations that I know well: Center for Mexican Philanthropy, *cemefi.org*; Africa Philanthropy Network, *africaphilanthropy.org*; and the Global Fund for Community Foundations, *globalfundcommunityfoundations.org*. For information on twenty-six countries and one region, see, Pamela Wiepking and Femida Handy, Editors. *The Palgrave Handbook of Global Philanthropy* (Hampshire, United Kingdom: Palgrave Macmillan, 2015).

Partnership beyond Collaboration

With potential philanthropic partners at the local level, US international grantmakers can now work as peer partners with local grantmakers on the basis of shared values and goals. Such partnerships enable you to reorient your grantmaking approach to fit local strategies and programs. It also enables you to shift the locus of control from you as the external actor to the internal actors. You and your partners will be better equipped to tackle persistent ethical dilemmas of international grantmaking: dependency on external donors and lack of sustainability.

Ethical International Grantmaking: Lessons from the Past

Over more than one hundred years of US international grantmaking, you can find many examples of how program staff, with the support of presidents and trustees, embarked on expanding their programs or supporting projects around the world.[47]

These examples are instructive of how grantmakers and their international partners assessed and acted on ethical challenges that are still relevant in our era.[48] I chose to examine three specific cases in which ethical issues were an intrinsic guiding force in decision-making.

The Ford Foundation's 1972 decision by the president and board of trustees to continue grantmaking in South Africa under the ethically charged situation of apartheid resulted from extensive consultations of the New York-based staff with activists, scholars, and officials primarily in the country and the region. This decision laid the groundwork for US

---

[47] See, for example Merle Curti, *American Philanthropy Abroad* (New Brunswick, New Jersey: Rutgers University Press, 1963); Richard Magat, *The Ford Foundation at Work: Philanthropic Choices, Methods and Styles* (New York and London: Plenum Publishing Company Limited, 1979); Patricia L Rosenfield, *A World of Giving: Carnegie Corporation of New York—a Century of International Philanthropy* (New York: PublicAffairs, 2014); William S. Moody with Priscilla Lewis, ed., *Staying the Course: Reflections on 40 Years of Grantmaking at the Rockefeller Brothers Fund* (London: Alliance Publishing Trust, 2014); Rockefeller Archive Center, "The Rockefeller Foundation: A Digital History," *rockfound.rockarch.org*.

[48] An instructive interview on an international grantmaker's decades of ethical grantmaking: Carolyn Hartnell, "Interview—Bill Carmichael," *Alliance Magazine*, 14, No. 2 (June 1, 2009), *alliancemagazine.org/interview/interview-bill-carmichael*.

Dead-End Philanthropy

Tade Aina (currently executive director, Program for African Social and Governance Research, Nairobi, Kenya, former director Carnegie Corporation's Higher Education in Africa program and former Ford Foundation Regional Representative, East Africa and Acting Regional Representative Middle East and North Africa) flagged an ongoing problem: external funders continue to support local nonprofits, despite their precarious financial situations (interview, August 20, 2017). Aina pointed out that even though such local organizations and critical movements (women's rights, environmental justice, etc.) permeate the African continent, the issue of sustainability has never been satisfactorily resolved.

Aina sees this as endemic to the structural context of many local settings throughout Africa and the *Global South*. He believes that now is the time to examine the local roots of these organizations and movements so that the grants don't lead to "dead-end philanthropy." To reduce dependence on outside resources, an often-proposed solution is providing endowment support. Aina regretted that this is rarely considered for local nonprofits in developing countries.

grantmakers and local actors to band together to bring about the end of apartheid rule.[49]

The second example I have in mind, the International Health Policy Program case reflects how US grantmaking organizations and international agencies working with and guided by local grantees across universities and government ministries can bring about sustainable policy change.[50]

Finally, the efforts to establish the Global Fund for Community Foundations illustrate how US grantmaking organizations together with international and local partners drew on historical experience and respect for local context to act on evidence, not impulse, when they

---

[49] Stephen Golub, "Battling Apartheid, Building a New South Africa," in *Many Roads of Justice*, McClymont and Golub, eds., 19-54; Ford Foundation History Project Team, "Continuity Amidst Change: The History of the Ford Foundation in South Africa, 1952–1993," (Sleepy Hollow, New York: Rockefeller Archive Center, January 2014).
[50] Ralph Andreano. *The International Health Policy Program* (Madison, Wisconsin: The University of Madison Press, 2001).

established a new global organization aimed at promoting sustainable local grantmaking.[51]

Here are some of the main lessons learned from these cases that every *ethical international grantmaker* should have in mind:

Successful implementation results from active consultation and engagement with a wide range of local actors and like-minded external donors. Past experiences confirm that the key to success and sustainability of an international project is for the US grantmakers to fully understand the local and regional dimensions of the project and to work diligently to establish trust with colleagues in the country or countries involved. As an international grantmaker, you should strive to follow the lead of local grantees in providing the most helpful support for their situation.

The importance of seeking and listening to multiple perspectives, along with developing an evidence base when planning a new initiative, cannot be overstated. Extensive consultations with local partners—experts and advisors, government decision-makers, partners, and potential beneficiaries—can lead to development of demand-driven models where local actors decide what is needed in their communities, what work should be undertaken, and why.

Greater involvement of local partners increases the likelihood of positive and sustainable outcomes. Partnerships based on consultation and engagement with local actors often lead to a vibrant source of financial, intellectual, and peer support for any international grantmaker working at the community level. Such an approach facilitates transforming collaboration into partnership, thus, increasing the likelihood of achieving sustainability.

Principles Underlying the Proposed Framework for Ethical International Grantmaking

Because philanthropy does not consider itself a profession, it has not developed a standard code of ethics. Nonetheless, two of the main network institutions that serve the field of US philanthropy—Independent Sector (IS) and the Council on Foundations (COF)—have developed and published principles and guidelines for ethical grantmaking.

---

[51] Barry Knight and Andrew Milner, "What Does Community Philanthropy Look like? Case Studies on Community Philanthropy -1," Mott Foundation (March 4, 2014), 1. *globalfundcommunityfoundations.org/information/tag/barry-knight.*

IS's first report, published in 1991 and reissued in 2002, states the key elements of ethical practice for the nonprofit sector. The most provocative of these is the concept of *obedience to the unenforceable*. This entails obedience to a series of values and standards that go beyond those enforceable by law.[52] In 2015, IS issued a new edition presenting thirty-three principles for good governance and ethical practice, along with guidance for implementation.[53]

Specifically focused on reaching US and European international grant-makers, in 2005, the COF with its partner institution in Europe, the European Foundation Centre (EFC), established a Joint Working Group on Accountability for International Philanthropy.[54] Both had recognized that guidance on a broad definition of accountability would enhance the ethical effectiveness of international grantmaking. The intent was that every international donor should ask, "To whom is my organization responsible as it makes grants or develops projects across borders?"[55]

The working group members consulted widely with experts, grantees, and philanthropic partner organizations throughout Latin America, Europe, and Africa. Despite the considerable complexities of cross-border philanthropy, they reached consensus on a set of principles and practices.[56]

Seven Principles of Accountability for International Philanthropy

1. Integrity

2. Understanding

3. Respect

4. Responsiveness

5. Fairness

[52] Independent Sector, "Obedience to the Unenforceable: Ethics and the Nation's Voluntary and Philanthropic Community," 1991, Revised 2002. 17-18. *efc.issuelab.org/resources/16107/16107.pdf.*
[53] Principles for Good Governance and Ethical Practice: A Guide for Charities and Foundations." 2015 edition. *independentsector.org/wp-content/uploads/2016/11/Principles2015-Web.pdf.*
[54] Joint Working Group of the Council on Foundations and the European Foundation Centre. "Principles of Accountability: an Aspirational Tool for International Donors." Council on Foundations and European Foundation Centre, April 2007. *cof.org/content/principles-accountability-international-philanthropy-0.*
[55] Joint Working Group, "Principles," 10.
[56] Joint Working Group, "Principles," 11-19 provide more details.

6. Cooperation and Collaboration

7. Effectiveness

These principles inform the following *good practice options*:

◆ Align your international philanthropy with your vision and mission

◆ Understand the context in which you operate

◆ Engage with others. Do not work in isolation

◆ Inform, listen, and respond

◆ Respect diversity, autonomy, and knowledge

◆ Build trust. Invest for the long term

◆ Ensure good governance

◆ Ensure good stewardship of philanthropic resources

◆ Assess, learn, and share knowledge

Suggested Framework for Ethical International Grantmaking Strategies

Drawing on the experiences of international grantmakers and the consensus around principles and best-practice options, this framework is action-oriented. It builds on an experience-based framework developed by my colleagues and myself. It is also informed by best development practices that empower local communities to set and implement their community agenda in partnership with others.[57]

The intent of this framework is to help make the most ethically effective use of your and your grantee partners' scarce resources of money, time, and trust. While the questions are not posed in ethical terms, they do reflect the attributes discussed throughout this chapter.

---

[57] Rosenfield et al, "Ethical Dimensions," 51-52; Daniel C. Taylor and Carl E. Taylor, *Just and Lasting Change: When Communities Own Their Futures, Second Edition* (Baltimore: Johns Hopkins University Press, 2016); Asian Development Bank Study Team (Irfani Darma and Anggun Susilo), *Toward Mainstreaming and Sustaining Community Driven Development in Indonesia: Understanding Local Initiatives and the Transition from the National Rural Community Empowerment Program to the Village Law*, Asian Development Bank January 1, 2016, *adb.org/sites/default/files/publication/178696/mainstreaming--cdd-Indonesia.pdf.*

Project Identification

◆ What other work has been done on this theme? In this local setting? In the region? Elsewhere? What are the lessons learned from
that work? Are those lessons applicable? If other work has been
done, what is your comparative advantage in choosing to work
again on this theme?

◆ Have you made a preliminary site visit to meet with local donors,
scholars, activists, and decision-makers to learn about the issues
they have identified that need more attention? Will they find it
useful to have an outside partner?

◆ How do your project's aims and objectives fit with those of local
funders and local/national policies? Have you identified potential
partners? Have you met with them? Are people already working
on this theme? With whom might you work or encourage to work
on this theme?

Project Development

◆ Have you shared with your local partners and potential grantees
the level of resources and initial timeframe for the project? Have
you discussed the likelihood of extending beyond the first round
of funding? Have you discussed preparing a memorandum of
understanding, no matter how modest the undertaking?

◆ Once you've established a working relationship with likely partners, have you encouraged them to prepare a project prospectus?
Have you discussed together the kind of guidance that would be
most helpful?

◆ Have you also discussed the proposed project with other grantmakers with whom the local team and you might want to work?

◆ Have you made sure that everyone is on the same page about
the: timeframe for the planning process; submission, review, and
decision-making process at your organization (and the possi-
bilities for delays and further questions and possible deferral or
turndown); plans for site visits; timeframe for the program or project; opportunities for outreach and dissemination; likely interest
in scaling up; and, often the most sensitive aspect, an approach to
internal and external intermediate and final evaluations?

◆ Have you thoroughly discussed criteria for evaluation, especially the indicators for achieving the goals, aims, and objectives? Have you together considered what knowledge will be useful, even if those indicators are not uniformly positive? Have you discussed the key elements required for sustainability? Is there a need for any special training or refresher courses on any of these points? Is there an interest in working with local consultants or others who can assist with any of these aspects?

Project Implementation

◆ Do you have a memorandum of understanding agreed upon by all involved? Such a statement will enable this phase—while always allowing for the possibility of unintended consequences—to be productive for both the external and internal actors. This will help ensure a shared understanding by all involved about the part-nership and the project. It will also facilitate respectful and fair handling of disagreements, should they arise.

◆ Has the project developed targeted communication approaches for outreach to the local community, policymakers, other funders, and others elsewhere, including the US philanthropic community? Is there a team member tasked with the responsibility, especially for reaching out to the project community or constituency?

◆ Who has the responsibility for ensuring the effective functioning of the team? Are team-building and team-maintaining proce-dures in place?

◆ Will you be the only program staff visiting? If not, how will you make sure that others from your organization or other partners respect the same principles and actions that you do?

◆ Will you assume responsibility for working with the team to ensure that the monitoring and evaluation are conducted in the fairest and most respectful manner, without value judgment the part of the external evaluator, and with open communication about areas that are succeeding and those involving more difficulties? What are the mechanisms for continuing the successful efforts and addressing the problematic ones? Do you have access to additional resources in order to tackle any unanticipated issues?

◆ Considering the broadened definition of public trust, will you assist your in-country partners to visit to the United States and elsewhere to share their results and to make new contacts for future activities? Will you invite them to meet with your board, president, and other staff members?

End of Project Evaluation and the Decision to Continue or Terminate

If the earliest discussions led to agreement on the evaluation approach and criteria for continuing or terminating work, including, as appropriate, a carefully conceived exit strategy, then this part of the work will be less anxiety-ridden. Instead, it will reveal what worked and what didn't, which new lessons were learned and older ones confirmed.

This may seem unduly idealistic, but when respect, fairness, and trust are the operative criteria for a relationship, whatever the outcomes and final decisions, the project will have succeeded in building a positive working relationship with your local partners, along with developing capacity for the next activity. This kind of success will likely open new opportunities for your international grantmaking.

Perhaps the most challenging aspect at this stage is to understand the nature of what can be sustained and how. This is hard to determine in advance. If all the relevant partners—including those on the local level—have been part of the process, then the team can identify what aspects to sustain and how.

At this stage, you and your partners might have the opportunity to extend the impact of the lessons learned, i.e., go to scale. If policymakers or other leaders have been involved in the work, they might request this. They may, however, also ask you for additional resources. It is important to discuss, at an earlier stage, whether this might be a possibility or whether they will need to identify local resources for this purpose.

Documentation, Dissemination, Outreach, and Next Steps

Documentation and outreach should be relatively straightforward if these efforts have been ongoing. Again, for meeting the broadened public trust criterion, depending on the results, you and the team members may decide to reach out to wider-than-planned audiences. Such audiences, both within and outside the country, could include scholars, policymakers, and/or international, intergovernmental, or nongovernmental organizations. Your organization might wish to feature the project's outcomes on its website. You and your partners might want to share the results with international nonprofits and publications.

At the project's end, you and your local partners will have established a trust-based relationship. This will certainly help you identify opportunities for future joint activities, possibly in unanticipated ways.

Challenges in Applying this Ethical Framework

Internally, issues may arise in your organization and externally, with domestic and overseas partners, that impede your using the framework. For example, this process may take more time at the early stages and lead to delays in grant submission.

Working in partnership with local actors, both funders and grantees, could change the nature of grantmaking. Local actors will take the lead in shaping the agenda for local action and local funding. Your role will be to align your program strategies to reinforce their efforts. Such a change will positively inform ethical and effective grantmaking.

You may encounter some colleagues—for instance, trustees—who may be concerned about the metrics for measuring success with this change. You should be able to offer reassurance that ethical grantmaking does not imply that outcomes will be less tangible. To the contrary, as you and the team will have planned the work, tangible, quantifiable outcomes should result. Descriptive qualitative analysis, if also planned for from the beginning, will help in assessing the intangible outcomes.

Despite the many questions, this framework may actually be easier to use in smaller grantmaking organizations where staff may have wide scope of action; larger institutions may have more levels of decision-making and less flexibility. Nonetheless, engaging with the framework is a way to encourage each program staff team or individual officer to act in an informed, intrapreneurial manner. This can enhance the vibrancy and effectiveness of an institution. The early history of US grantmaking organizations vividly describes the successful application of this approach.[58]

While the framework pulls together accumulated best practices of many international grantmakers, you will likely identify new concerns and shape your own approach as you customize your use of the framework. There is not yet an extensive literature with grantmakers explicitly discussing the ethics of grantmaking, international or domestic, let alone the use of guidelines. To contribute your experiences to this knowledge

---

[58] See, Rockefeller Archive Center, Rockefeller Centennial Website, especially the biography section.

base, you might consider keeping track of the ethical challenges and solutions in your international work.[59] By sharing your experiences with other grantmakers, you will help deepen understanding of best practices and encourage others to do the same. You will pave the way for achieving more ethically effective and sustainable results by US international grantmakers.

Note

In writing this chapter, I have benefited from the insights and experiences of a wide range of colleagues. I am especially grateful to: my Rockefeller Archive Center colleagues—Jack Meyers, James Allen Smith, Barbara Shubinski, Rachel Wimpee, Laura Miller, and Marissa Vassari; Andrea Johnson [Carnegie Corporation of New York (CCNY)]; Eleanor Lerman (formerly CCNY, who generously contributed her superior editing skills); William Carmichael [formerly, Ford Foundation (FF)]; Tada Aina (formerly CCNY and FF), Partnership for African Social and Governance Research; Daniel Taylor, Future Generations; and Deborah Rose, Harvard University FXB Center for Health and Human Rights. The recommendations and comments in this chapter do not represent official policy of the Rockefeller Archive Center. I am solely responsible for them and any errors.

---

[59] Illingworth et al, *Giving Well*, 4; Rosenfield et al, "Ethical Dimensions," 62-63.

Patricia Rosenfield, PhD

Patricia L. Rosenfield, PhD, Senior Fellow, Rockefeller Archives Center (RAC), Sleepy Hollow, New York, undertakes activities to connect practitioners and scholars of philanthropy. Her areas of focus include the history of the Ford Foundation, the role of US foundations in the early history of the HIV/AIDS, and foundation support for international fellowships and exchanges.

Before joining RAC, Patricia was at Carnegie Corporation of New York, first chairing its Strengthening Human Resources in Developing Countries Program and then directing the Carnegie Scholars Program. Earlier she served at the World Health Organization in Geneva, responsible for a global program on social and economic research on tropical diseases.

Patricia holds an AB *cum laude* from Bryn Mawr College, a PhD from Johns Hopkins University, and an Honorary Doctorate from Mahidol University, Bangkok. She has written on the history, practice, and ethics of philanthropy; approaches to interdisciplinary team science; international health; and economic development. Patricia is coeditor with Frank Kessel and Norman Anderson of *Expanding the Boundaries of Health and Social Science* (Oxford University Press, 2003) and an updated volume, *Interdisciplinary Research, Second Edition* (Oxford, 2008). She is the author of *A World of Giving: Carnegie Corporation of New York, A Century of International Grantmaking* (PublicAffairs, 2014).

Chapter Four

Mechanisms for International Grantmaking

Beth Kingsley

A US-based funder who wants to support charitable work in another country can choose between several available mechanisms. These include giving directly to a recognized 501(c)(3) organization that will carry out the activity, giving to an intermediary grantmaker, or making a grant directly to a foreign organization. Which approach is right depends on what kind of entity the funder is, what concerns motivate it, and what it wants to accomplish with the grant.

The legal issues that drive the choice of mechanism vary for different funders. An individual or company likely wants to be able to take a tax deduction for the charitable contribution. Private foundations will be concerned with avoiding excise taxes that can be triggered by improper or careless grantmaking. A public charity will want to preserve its 501(c)(3) tax exemption. And all will want to ensure that their funds are used for the intended purpose, not diverted to private uses, or used in violation of US antiterrorism, anti-money laundering, or other laws, and consistent with the laws of the country where the activity will take place. This chapter focuses on the first set of concerns, rooted in provisions of the US tax code. **Chapters Five** through **Ten** address other important legal considerations.

US 501(c)(3) Organizations

A relatively straightforward option for funding international charitable activity is to make a grant to a 501(c)(3) organization that carries out the work directly.

US Charities with International Programs

A US public charity—that is, an organization exempt under § 501(c)(3) of the US tax code that is not classified as a private foundation—may have international programs. Indeed, a charity can qualify for that status under US law even if all of its activities are carried out in another county. For instance, the key case establishing this point concerned a nonprofit organized under US law that operated a school in France, *Bilingual Montessori School of Paris, Inc.*, 75 T.C. 480 (1980). Because it was a US nonprofit entity and operated for educational purposes as a school, it was eligible to be treated as a 501(c)(3) public charity.

Private foundations may also operate internationally, but for purposes of this discussion we presume that most foundations are more likely to want to fund operations than to conduct their own program activities.

More typically, a US charity may have both US and international programs. It may operate in one or many foreign countries. Because it is a US 501(c)(3), donations are eligible for tax deductions as charitable contributions. Private foundations and DAF sponsors can make grants to the US public charity without employing special procedures. And all of these funders can designate their contributions to support specific programs. (As we'll see later, earmarking a contribution to be transferred to a different organization carrying out that same program creates legal headaches.)

Foreign Organizations with 501(c)(3) Rulings

Charities that are organized in foreign countries may also have an IRS ruling recognizing them as 501(c)(3)s. Contributions to these organizations are not deductible as charitable contributions for US income tax purposes. However, once a foreign charity is recognized by the IRS as 501(c)(3), public charities, private foundations, and DAF sponsors may make grants to them as to any other US public charity. There is no need to employ the special procedures that usually apply to grants

Charities can take different legal forms. Probably most familiar is the nonprofit corporation, but a charity can also be established as a trust or even a fund within another organization. For a corporation to claim a charitable contribution deduction for international activities, the recipient charity must be a nonprofit corporation rather than a trust, fund, or *"community chest."* (No, that's not just a term from Monopoly!)

to foreign organizations. (Expenditure responsibility and equivalency determinations are discussed below in the context of direct cross-border grants. Details on each of these processes are in **Chapters Five** and **Six**.)

The downside for a foreign organization of having US recognition of 501(c)(3) status is that the organization must file tax returns like any other 501(c)(3). This includes the annual Form 990 information return, as well as the 990-T if the organization has unrelated business taxable income. This filing obligation continues for the existence of the organization. Even if the group stops receiving US funding, the IRS expects the Form 990 and will impose penalties for late or nonfiling. There is no mechanism for an organization to surrender its 501(c)(3) status. The foreign organization will have United States filing obligations even if it never again expects to receive funding from the United States. If it loses its broad public support and becomes a private foundation, it will almost certainly not receive further US-source funding but will be subject to an array of excise taxes if it does not comply with the special rules governing private foundations.

What Is a Donor Advised Fund?

A donor advised fund, often referred to as a DAF, is a fund maintained by a public charity, known as the *sponsoring organization*. It is a fund that is separately identified by reference to the contributions of one or more donors, and with respect to which a donor (or a donor's designee) has the right to advise the sponsoring organization about investment or distribution of the funds in the account. Although technically the donor does not have the right to direct how funds will be used, a donor's advice is usually given great weight. In this chapter, we'll use *DAF* to refer to the giving mechanism or fund, and *DAF sponsor* or *sponsoring organization* to refer to the public charity that houses one or more DAFs. When we talk about rules that apply to a DAF sponsor, we mean a DAF sponsor using funds from the DAF. Those rules won't generally apply to the sponsoring organization if it is using other non-DAF funds it may have.

Organizations Automatically Treated as 501(c)(3)s

Certain international organizations may be automatically recognized as tax-exempt under § 501(c)(3). This can result from provisions of a tax treaty between the United States and the foreign country, or because of the nature of the organization itself.

Tax treaties can provide for mutual recognition of the exempt status of charities in the countries that are party to them. For instance, the US-Canada tax treaty provides that a Canadian registered charity will automatically be deemed to be a 501(c)(3) organization, without requiring it to file any application. However, Canadian charities are not automatically treated as public charity, so they would still need to demonstrate that they qualify as a public charity and not a private foundation. This can take the form of a ruling from the IRS, which allows a funder, private foundation or DAF funder, to treat the organization as a public charity, or can be done as part of an equivalency determination (discussed below and in **Chapter Six**).

Churches, as well as their integrated auxiliaries and a convention or association of churches, are also considered automatically exempt under § 501(c)(3). Churches are also automatically treated as public charities. However, as a funder you would probably want to conduct your own inquiry to make sure that the organization genuinely qualifies as a church. The IRS looks at a fourteen-part list of characteristics to determine whether an organization is a church.[60]

Fiscal Sponsors

A fiscal sponsor is a recognized US public charity that provides a means to get tax-favored support to a program or entity that does not have its own 501(c)(3) ruling. Fiscal sponsorship can take many forms. For example, fiscal sponsorship may be a solution for US funders to support new organizations that are seeking 501(c)(3) status or can serve as incubators for projects not yet ready to stand on their own.[61]

In the international context, a fiscal sponsor may be a recognized charity that *adopts* an international project. The project is then carried out as part of the organization's own program. The project's receipts and expenses are carried on the books of the sponsor, and its financial and programmatic activity is included in the sponsor's Form 990. From a technical legal perspective, this is actually no different from a standard US charity with international operations. It is likely to be considered a fiscal sponsorship when the impetus for setting up the arrangement comes from a group of individuals interested in carrying out the project. Rather than create a new legal entity to house their work, they establish

---

[60] *See* Publication 1828, Tax Guide for Churches and Religious Organizations.
[61] A great source of more information on fiscal sponsorship in general is *fiscalsponsorship.com*.

a relationship with the fiscal sponsor. The funder's direct relationship is likely with the people carrying out the project, and it can be easy to slip into thinking about them as being the grantee. However, in this type of sponsorship, it is the fiscal sponsor who is being funded and carrying out the activities.

Another type of fiscal sponsorship is a *regranting* relationship. You may sometimes hear this described as a *conduit* relationship, but that is not how the sponsorship should be structured; the sponsor must not be a *mere conduit* which is legally understood just to pass funds along to the sponsored organization without exercising any discretion or control. In this type of sponsorship, there are two legal entities: a US charity that serves as a fiscal sponsor, and a sponsored organization that receives subgrants (or regrants) from the charity that accepts funding to support the sponsored organization's activities. The sponsor must have ultimate discretion and control over the use of the funds and may not be legally required to transmit them to the sponsored entity. This kind of fiscal sponsorship is actually a way of relying on an intermediary grantmaking organization.

Intermediary Grantmaking Organizations

Using an intermediary organization to make international grants can be very convenient for a funder. That is, the funder makes a contribution to a US organization which acts as an *intermediary*, and is then able to use the funding to support the international organization. Because the intermediary is recognized as a US public charity, an individual or corporation can claim a charitable contribution deduction, and a private foundation or DAF sponsor is not required to exercise any special oversight over the grant. The flip side of this convenience is that the donor must relinquish a degree of control. As you'll see from the discussion that follows, the contribution cannot simply be earmarked to be passed through to a foreign entity.

Friends of Organizations

Funders who want to support the work of a foreign charity often establish what is known as a *Friends of* organization—so called because these groups are often named *Friends of* [the name of the foreign charity]. A funder wishing to support program work in the foreign country may make grants to this *Friends of* organization which can then fund the work and take responsibility for legal compliance in the use of the funds.

Key to making this arrangement work is that the donation must actually be made to the US entity. If the funds are earmarked so that the recipient is required to transfer them to the foreign entity, then the intermediary is not considered to be the actual recipient of the funding. The IRS will ignore the intermediary and treat the grant as if it were made to the foreign charity. This would obviously eliminate the benefits of working with the recognized US charity as an intermediary, so it is important to make sure things are set up correctly. You'll see that similar issues apply to any US intermediary grantmaking organization, but it can be particularly tricky with a *Friends of* organization that typically supports only a single international charity.

An old (but still valid) IRS ruling, Rev. Rul. 66-79, 1966-1 C.B. 48, outlines how a *Friends of* organization may be set up and operated so that donations are treated as made to the US entity and not as improperly earmarked for the non-US organization. This compliance road map was set out in the bylaws of the organization in question in that ruling:

◆ The board of the organization should have exclusive power to make grants for the purposes expressed in the organization's charter or articles;

◆ Grants may be made to any organization organized and operated exclusively for charitable, scientific, or educational purposes within the meaning of section 501(c)(3), whether or not it has a ruling to that effect from the IRS;

◆ The board should review all funding requests from other organizations, require that the request specify how funds will be used, and authorize payment of the funds to the approved grantee;

◆ Grantees must furnish a periodic accounting to show that the funds were spent for the purposes approved by the board; and

◆ The board may, in its absolute discretion, refuse to make any grants for any of the requested purposes.

If these elements are met, then the organization may solicit funds for a specific board-approved project to be conducted by a foreign entity. However, the board must retain the right to withdraw approval of the grant and use the funds for other charitable, educational, or scientific purposes. The fact that the board may withdraw approval of a particular grant should be clearly communicated to all donors, and the *Friends of* organization should not accept contributions earmarked so that they must, in any event, be transferred to the foreign entity.

Contributions to a *Friends of* organization may be restricted as to purpose, but the organization must be free to accomplish that purpose by other means, such as making a grant to a different entity or conducting activity directly itself, should it so decide. The critical point is that the *Friends of* organization must have full control of donated funds and discretion as to their use so that the donation can be treated as actually made to the US entity and not earmarked for transmittal to a foreign organization.

A funder is generally entitled to rely on an IRS ruling issued to a *Friends of* organization. However, you must be careful not to add earmarking language, such as in a grant letter. If you direct the *Friends of* organization to transfer the contributed funds to the foreign entity you want to support, the transaction is likely to become a conduit arrangement. The *Friends of* organization should have appropriate language available for donors; indeed, it should have specific language in any solicitation materials that establishes that the *Friends of* organization will have full discretion and control over the funds. However, we all know that it is not unheard of for an organization *to move away* over time from the processes they adopted when they were established. To protect against making a *conduit* grant that is treated as direct donation to the foreign charity, you should review any solicitation materials to make sure they don't slip into earmarking. You may also want to conduct an inquiry to verify that the *Friends of* organization is operating consistent with the requirements outlined above.

Donor Advised Funds

Another mechanism for international grantmaking is the donor advised fund, or DAF, housed at a public charity, which is known as the DAF sponsor. A DAF represents a different approach to allowing a US funder to support an organization (foreign or domestic) that does not itself have a 501(c)(3) ruling. Unsurprisingly, similar rules relating to conduits and earmarking apply as in the *Friends of* organizations context.

Historically, DAFs were not defined in the tax code. They were funds maintained by public charities that would allow donors (or their designees) to provide advice or suggestions about the use of the funds— hence the name. Donors received the benefits of making a donation to a public charity but could continue to have a voice in how the money would be invested and ultimately disbursed. Some organizations were effectively in the business of operating DAFs, which in the eyes of some critics allowed donors to enjoy the benefits of a private foundation whose grantmaking they could control without having to comply with any of the relatively burdensome foundation rules. In the 2006 Pension Protection Act, Congress formally defined DAFs and imposed some restrictions on the kinds of grants they could make. Thus, a DAF sponsor seeking to make direct international grants must follow a process similar to those available to a private foundation (as discussed below).

But from the donor's perspective, a DAF at a public charity is a way to offload responsibility for oversight of a foreign grant while receiving all the tax benefits of giving to a US charity. As with a *Friends of* organization, you should make sure that a donation to a DAF is not earmarked to be regranted to a foreign entity. The DAF sponsoring organization must have discretion and control over the use (and investment) of the funds, and it is not legally required to follow your suggestions about subsequent disbursements. The DAF sponsor may commit to taking your advice into consideration, and as a matter of good donor relations, these organizations rarely disregard a donor's wishes. But they do remain legally free to do so, which means that if you want to rely on a DAF, you need to be willing to give up that degree of control.

Before making a donation to a DAF (which is an irrevocable gift to the DAF sponsoring organization under US law), you should also verify that the sponsoring organization is willing to make international grants. It is much simpler to support a recognized US public charity, so some DAF sponsoring organizations limit their grantmaking to US 501(c)(3)s. Also, because the DAF sponsor takes on an additional compliance burden when making international grants, they are likely to charge a fee against the fund to cover the associated costs.

Restricted Grants

Another way to use an intermediary grantmaking organization is to make a donation (to a public charity) that is restricted to be used for certain purposes—with the intention, of course, that the purpose will be accomplished by granting the funds to a foreign organization. Restricted grants may be combined with funds from other sources intended to support a particular program area. Of course, the purpose for which the funds are restricted must be consistent with the mission of the recipient organization, as well as with the requirements of § 501(c)(3).

In many ways this is similar to what a *Friends of* organization does. The difference is that a *Friends of* organization ordinarily only funds a single specific foreign entity, and usually its only function is to raise funds, make grants, and ensure that the funds are spent to accomplish charitable purposes. But the restricted grant can be made to any existing 501(c)(3) intermediary organization that is able to provide grants to organizations abroad and exercise adequate oversight over the use of those funds.

Similar restrictions apply as with any grant via an intermediary organization. The funds cannot be earmarked to be transmitted to a foreign organization, and the intermediary must have sufficient discretion and control—that it is free to redirect the funds to another recipient or otherwise accomplish the purposes for which the contribution was given.

Let's look at an example. Say a US donor wants to help build a school in a village in a country where educational resources are scarce. A US charity's mission is to promote early childhood education around the world, and it agrees that supporting this work would be consistent with its mission. If the donor makes a contribution to this charity and says that *this money is to be given to the organization in the village that intends to operate the school*, then the donation will be treated as given to the foreign entity. If the donor gives money to the US charity and says *this is to be used to promote education in Village X*, then the charity must use the funds for that purpose but is legally free to accomplish it by any appropriate means; therefore, the donation will qualify for a charitable tax deduction in the United States if the donor is an individual or taxable corporation.

Direct Cross-Border Grants

As we've said above, both private foundations and DAF sponsors are allowed to make direct grants to international grantees, but they must follow specific procedures to avoid incurring penalty taxes. Of course, individuals and companies are also legally allowed to make direct gifts to foreign organizations, but they cannot claim a charitable contribution tax deduction. For these donors, the US charitable vehicles described above are usually more appealing—that is, *Friends of* organizations, grantmaking intermediaries, or a family or corporate foundation. And of course those charitable organizations will themselves then make a direct cross-border grant, and so will need to understand the applicable rules. The discussion below gives an overview of issues related to the funding mechanisms, but international funders should also bear in mind the need to conduct proper vetting of grantees and consider anti-money laundering and antiterrorist financing measures, discussed in **Chapters Seven** to **Nine**.

Consideration for All Funders

For any funder that is an organization (as opposed to an individual), the governing board has a fiduciary duty to ensure that the organization's funds are used for charitable purposes, consistent with its mission. The precise parameters of the board's duty will vary depending on the form of organization (e.g., nonprofit corporation or trust) but the fundamental obligation applies.[62] This does not mean that the board must approve every single grant that is made, but it should exercise enough oversight over a grantmaking program to know how the organization's funds are being used and to verify that any foreign grants (or really all grants) further the mission.

As we've discussed, to preserve the funder's tax benefits a grantmaking organization must exercise discretion and control over its grants to ensure they are used for charitable purposes and should not accept funds earmarked for transmittal to an international grantee. This is important as a matter of responsible grantmaking in any case. The grantmaking organization should also maintain adequate records to demonstrate why grants were made and how the funds were used.

Private foundations have two options when making a direct grant to a foreign organization that doesn't have IRS recognition of its 501(c)(3) public charity status: expenditure responsibility and equivalency determination (explained below). Public charities are not subject to these specific requirements, but responsible grantmaking suggests they should follow similar (if less onerous) procedures.

DAF sponsors, unlike public charities and private foundations, are outright prohibited from making a grant to an individual person, whether in the United States or abroad, without triggering punitive excise taxes. Grants to organizations are allowed so long as they are made for charitable purposes (within the meaning of the tax code) *and* the DAF

---

[62] Technically, some organizational forms, such as the unincorporated association, may not impose fiduciary duties on the governing body. However, in all cases, the organization will have a legal obligation to spend funds consistent with the purposes for which they were raised.

sponsoring organization exercises expenditure responsibility (or the grant is made to a recognized public charity). The IRS has indicated that a DAF sponsor may rely on an equivalency determination the same way a private foundation can.

Foundations: Expenditure Responsibility

Expenditure responsibility, or ER, is a special process that allows a private foundation or DAF sponsor to make a single grant to a specific grantee that does not have a ruling that it is a 501(c)(3) public charity. This includes foreign charities unless they have received an IRS 501(c)(3) ruling. ER requires a pre-grant inquiry to provide assurance that the grantee will use the grant for appropriate purposes; a written grant agreement that includes specific terms about use of the funds, prohibited uses, and required reports; reporting back from the grantee to the foundation about the use of funds; and reporting from the foundation to the IRS on its 990-PF as long as the grant is still open.

The specific requirements to make an ER grant are quite detailed, and discussed in depth in **Chapter Five**. But for purposes of choosing a funding mechanism, what we should recognize is that ER can be very burdensome, and that burden is not much reduced when you make subsequent grants to a prior grantee. Further, ER requires that you prohibit the use of funds for certain purposes. Some of these are not problematic; it should not be surprising that charitable funds cannot be used for non-charitable purposes, or to influence specific elections for public office. However, an ER grant must also include a prohibition on using the funds for lobbying or voter registration. In contrast, a grant to a public charity (or organization that has been determined to be a public charity equivalent) may not be earmarked for those uses, but does not have to affirmatively include those prohibitions. There is even a rule, known as the *project grant rule*, that allows a single project that includes both lobbying and nonlobbying components to be funded by several different private foundations without any single foundation being considered to have earmarked its grant for lobbying.

Foundations: Equivalency Determination

The other mechanism for a private foundation or DAF sponsor to make a direct international grant is by conducting equivalency determination, or ED. The organization can permissibly make the grant without exercising ER if it makes a good faith determination that the grantee is the equivalent of a US public charity. This can require a substantial amount of work. The funder is, in effect, making the same determination that the IRS does when it reviews an application for tax exemption, complicated by the fact that the laws of the foreign country may not impose the same kind of restrictions on activities of a nonprofit as does US law. The regulations do create a presumption that a determination is made in good faith if it is based on the written opinion of a qualified tax practitioner.

In any case, whether the determination is made by the organization on its own or in reliance on an opinion of counsel, it can then be relied upon by the respective organization for making repeated grants. For future years, the information just needs to be updated. The grantee can be treated as a US public charity, so there is no need to prohibit the use of funds for specific activities. Remember, though, that in any case, a private foundation can't make a grant that is specifically earmarked for lobbying, to influence the outcome of an election, or for voter registration.[63] This is different from having to affirmatively prohibit using funds for those activities. If the grant is not earmarked, the grantee may choose to use grant funds for those purposes, consistent with any limitations imposed by its own tax-exempt status.

Grants to a foreign organization with an ED can easily be made for general support, or for any permissible activity of the grantee, including fundraising. Also, once you've made the determination, it's usually pretty easy to update. You need to verify that the grantee's governing documents and operations are not materially changed, and if there is any new program activity you need to vet it for compliance with 501(c)(3) requirements. If the organization's public charity status is based on its funding sources (rather than its status such as being a church or a school), that financial information needs to be updated and reviewed. For further details on ED, please see **Chapter Six**.

International Organizations

As we've seen, grants made by a private foundation to an organization, whether foreign or domestic, must be to a public charity (or a public charity equivalent) or made using the ER process. The regulations create an exception that is particularly relevant in the international context.

A foundation can treat a grantee as a public charity if it is a foreign government or an *agency or instrumentality* of a foreign government, *or* if

---

[63] A foundation can make a grant for voter registration if the grantee meets certain additional requirements, set out in Code § 4945(f).

it has been designated by executive order as an *international organiza-tion*. There is no requirement of further inquiry about the organization's charitable status. Even if it were to be disqualified from 501(c)(3) status, your foundation could make a grant to one of these international orga-nizations on the same terms as if you had conducted an ED, or as if the grantee had obtained a 501(c)(3) public charity ruling from the IRS.

Organizations that have been designated as qualifying international organizations include the United Nations, the European Space Agency, and the Global Fund to Fight AIDS, Tuberculosis, and Malaria. A com-plete list can be found at *uscode.house.gov*. You'll see a list of all currently designated international organizations, from the African Development Bank to the World Trade Organization. There is also a list of previously designated groups whose status has since been revoked by a subse-quent executive order. In case of doubt, you can always ask a prospective grantee to provide a copy of the relevant executive order and then just check to make sure it hasn't been reversed.

Grants by Public Charities

Public charities do not have to follow the specific rules that apply to pri-vate foundations. That is, they do not have to either make an equivalency determination or exercise expenditure responsibility in order to make a grant to a foreign organization. However, like all 501(c)(3)s they must ensure that their funds are spent in furtherance of their (charitable, edu-cational, religious, or scientific) mission.

Although we can't point to a specific regulation or ruling that says this, it is widely accepted that a public charity is protected if it follows the rules that apply to private foundations, which are more strictly regulated. So can a public charity follow the ER process in its international grantmak-ing? Well, yes, but some of the requirements for ER reflect rules that only apply to private foundations—for instance, the prohibition on lobbying, or use of funds for voter registration. Unlike foundations, public chari-ties can engage in or fund a limited amount of lobbying and can do (or support) voter registration drives without limit, so long as they comply with rules about 501(c)(3) nonpartisanship. Also, because ER reporting is only required for foundations, there is no specific mechanism for a charity to report on outstanding ER grants to the IRS, other than the gen-eral reporting on grants that is part of its Form 990.

That said, the ER process suggests useful steps for a public charity seek-ing to make a direct international grant:

Advance Inquiry and Review of Documentation

You should make an advance inquiry to ensure that the grantee can be relied upon to use the funds for permissible purposes and to comply with all terms of the grant agreement. The extent of this inquiry can vary depending on your relationship with the grant recipient, but consider looking at governing documents, assess financial systems, and review financial and programmatic reports for prior years' programs.

A Written Grant Agreement

A written agreement should promote legal compliance and also clearly set out expectations for funder and grantee. At a minimum, it should require that funds be used for exclusively charitable purposes,[64] and prohibit noncharitable uses. Lobbying should be prohibited or allowed only to a specified extent.[65]

Grantee Reporting

The grantee should be required to report regularly on the use of funds. Reports should be sufficient to document that funds were used for charitable purposes. If any lobbying was permitted, the reports should also be sufficient to demonstrate that your money was only used for (direct or grassroots) lobbying to the extent allowed.

Form 990 Reporting

Foreign activities or grants can trigger special reporting requirements on Form 990, Schedule F. You should make sure that your grant process generates all the information needed to complete this schedule properly. And before making direct international grants, make sure you are comfortable disclosing publicly the information required on that schedule.

A public charity can also undertake an equivalency determination for an international grantee. This would make sense if you expect to have a long-term funding relationship, or if you want to make a general support grant or help fund infrastructure and capacity building. Since those facilities will support the overall operations of the grantee, you need to make sure that supporting the entire entity (as opposed to a specific charitable project) is an appropriate use of 501(c)(3) resources.

---

[64] "Charitable" here includes educational, religious, and other purposes included under § 501(c)(3).

[65] If you have elected to be covered by the expenditure test of § 501(h), regulations will over-allocate grants to a non-501(c)(3) to lobbying, and also to grassroots lobbying, unless you impose appropriate restrictions. This rule applies to domestic as well as international grants.

Picking the Best Course of Action

So, those are the options. But which one is best for you? The answer depends on what kind of funder is providing the funds, what their concerns are, their organizational capacity, mission, and comfort level with exercising oversight over grantees—or not exercising such oversight.

An individual (or company) who wants to claim a charitable contribution deduction for their gift will want to make their donation to a US 501(c)(3) public charity. That could be an organization that will itself carry out the work or an intermediary that can regrant funds to an international organization and exercise the required oversight. This can be a *Friends of* organization if one exists or a foundation, DAF sponsor, or public charity that is willing to make cross-border grants.

A private foundation or DAF sponsor's primary legal concern will likely be avoiding punitive excise taxes. For these funders, things are simple if there is a US public charity that conducts an international program consistent with the funder's interests. It's also straightforward if a foreign nonprofit organization has an IRS ruling that it qualifies under § 501(c)(3) and is a public charity, or if the organization has been designated by executive order, as discussed above.

If these easy cases don't apply, you'll have to choose between ER and ED. You can judge for yourself after reading **Chapters Five** and **Six**, but in general, ED is considered to be more work up front but likely to be easier for repeat grants in the future. As a result, ED is likely the preferred mechanism if you intend to have an ongoing relationship, making multiple grants to the foreign grantee. ED is probably the best option if you want to make a general support grant, or to support fundraising or other capacity-building activities of the recipient. Those are only appropriate things to fund with charitable grants if the organization whose capacity you'd be building is a 501(c)(3), or 501(c)(3) equivalent. (Technically, an ER grant can be for general support, but it must also be restricted to use for charitable purposes within the meaning of section 501(c)(3).) ED can also allow you to rely on the project grant rule to fund a project that includes a mix of lobbying and nonlobbying activities without having to expressly prohibit the use of your grant for lobbying.

ER, on the other hand, usually entails less work up front, but that work needs to be repeated for each ER grant. This makes ER a good candidate for a one-off grant. And it is the only option if the grantee can't qualify for equivalency. On the other hand, if you're making a grant for endowment, or a capital purchase, ER becomes less desirable because it requires ongoing reporting from the grantee (and from you to the IRS) over a period of many years.

While public charities are not subject to the specific rules about ER and ED, similar considerations will be relevant. A public charity should certainly be able to rely on an equivalency determination—that is, if it can make a good faith determination that the foreign grantee is a 501(c)(3) equivalent, the funder can make grants as to any other 501(c)(3) organization. This will facilitate repeat funding, and allow grants to be made without restriction, leaving the grantee with more flexibility to apply the funding. On the other hand, where the grantee is not a charity equivalent, you can still provide funding for specific charitable projects.

In any case, where a public charity is serving as a grantmaking intermediary, it should always remember to exercise discretion and control over the destination and use of its funds. Public charity grantors should not be mere *conduits* to foreign organizations, but must play the role of a responsible grantmaker.

A public charity also has the option of doing the work directly itself. But of course, establishing international operations can be a huge undertaking, and you may well decide that it is more effective to support the work of a foreign organization already on the ground in the area where you want to work.

Other Considerations

In picking the right mechanism, you'll also need to consider your own capacity. Do you have the staff and resources to take on direct international grants yourself? If that's a concern, then consider using an intermediary. An organization that is in the business of international grantmaking should already have procedures in place to carry out the necessary due diligence, employ appropriate documentation, receive and review reports, and comply with the various US laws that apply when sending funds internationally. Or if there is an appropriate US-based organization that has international operations, you could of course fund that.

In choosing between ER and ED, you should consider both your capacity as well as that of the grantee. Doing a full ED can entail a lot of work, and not every foreign organization will be able to jump through the necessary hoops. Even with a lot of support from a funder familiar with US law, gathering all the required information can be a daunting task—one not made any easier by the language barrier that may also be involved. ER may be more work for you, but it is likely easier for your grantee to comply with the restrictions on the specific funding you're providing than to have to pull together information about all its operations sufficient to support a determination that it's a public charity equivalent. On the other hand, if the grantee has a prospect of funding from multiple US sources, it may be worth it in the long run for them to go through the ED process.

Consider also whether the governing documents and policies of your organization impose any constraints on your choice of mechanism for funding international activities. Do the articles of incorporation, bylaws, declaration of trust, or other governing documents permit international grants? Even if these documents are drafted broadly enough to allow the activity, is it consistent with your organization's mission? Has the board of directors approved international grantmaking? This specific grant? And if the board does not approve specific grants, are they being made within parameters set by the board? You should ask these questions about international grantmaking generally, and about any specific grant.

Different mechanisms will also appeal to different funding styles. Some grantmakers want to have a high degree of control over how their funds are used. Others may not have the resources to exercise that level of oversight, or simply prefer a more hands-off approach.

Direct grantmaking both requires and allows the highest degree of control and oversight on the part of the funder. As you'll see later in **Chapter Five**, to exercise expenditure responsibility you have to both make an inquiry about the grantee before making a grant and stay involved in oversight of funds until the project is accomplished and fully reported on. In the case of grants for capital equipment or endowment, that oversight and reporting must continue for at least two years after the grant is made.

Once an equivalency determination has been made, this level of oversight is not required. The same is true of a grant to a foreign organization with a 501(c)(3) letter, or to a US charity with international operations. With these grantees, the degree of oversight is left to your discretion. Grants can be restricted to specific uses, detailed reports required, and deviations from budgeted amount may require your advance approval.[66] At the other extreme, you can choose just to write a check to the charity

---

[66] Please note I'm talking here about what's allowed, and not suggesting that this degree of micro-managing is a desirable funding practice.

with no restriction as to use and no requirement of reporting back. Most funders, of course, will land somewhere in the middle.

Finally, using an intermediary grantmaker transfers to that intermediary the responsibility for oversight, but also requires giving up a degree of control. As discussed above, for a *Friends of* or other intermediary relationship to work under applicable tax rules, the donor may not require that their funds be transferred to a specific noncharitable recipient (that includes a foreign organization not formally recognized as a charity under US law). You have to be willing to trust the *discretion and control* of the intermediary, who must be legally free to accomplish the purposes of the grant however they deem best.

There is surely not a single *best* mechanism for international grantmaking, and in any given case there may not be a single obvious best choice. Every approach has its burdens and benefits. But by carefully considering the implications of each option, you can arrive at the course of action that meets your needs and most effectively accomplishes your mission.

Beth Kingsley

Beth Kingsley is an attorney at Harmon, Curran, Spielberg + Eisenberg, LLP where she represents nonprofit organizations and political campaigns, providing a full range of general counsel services to a variety of nonprofits including private foundations, associations, community-based groups, national and international public interest organizations, and political organizations. Her expertise includes state and federal tax exemption as well as the laws governing advocacy.

Beth cochairs the subcommittee on Politics and Lobbying Activities of the Exempt Organizations Committee of the ABA Tax Section and is a regular contributor to the journal *Taxation of Exempts*. She has a BA from Oberlin College and JD from Georgetown University Law Center.

Chapter Five

Tools for Direct International Grantmaking: Expenditure Responsibility

John Bennett and David Shevlin

As discussed in the preceding chapter, certain grants by private foundations, as well as certain grants by sponsoring organizations of donor advised funds (DAFs),[67] require the private foundation or DAF grantor to follow specific procedures designed to ensure that these grants are spent solely for the charitable purposes for which they are made. These procedures are referred to in the tax code as expenditure responsibility (ER).[68] A private foundation or DAF grantor that properly exercises ER will not be responsible (i.e., liable for excise taxes) if, subsequently, an issue arises with the use of its grant.

The ER rules set forth a specific and detailed process for private foundation and DAF grantors to follow before a grant is made, while grant funds are in use, and at the end of the grant period, in order to ensure that the grant is used only for its intended purposes and is not diverted for other, noncharitable uses. The ER rules also prescribe procedures for private foundation and DAF grantors to follow if they become aware of a diversion, or other improper use, of grant funds.

---

[67] While it is the sponsoring organization of a DAF that makes each DAF grant, we use the vernacular term *donor advised fund* (DAF) in this chapter to refer to sponsoring organizations.

[68] ER is defined in section 4945(h) of the Internal Revenue Code of 1986, as amended (the "Code") and further described in the Treasury Regulations at section 53.4945-5(b).

This chapter describes the circumstances in which ER is required, walks you through each step of the ER process in detail and provides practical tips for you as a private foundation or DAF grantor preparing to exercise ER in connection with a grant.

When Expenditure Responsibility Is Required

As a general matter, a grant by a private foundation or a DAF to an organization that is not recognized by the IRS as a public charity will be deemed a "taxable expenditure" (in the case of a private foundation) or a "taxable distribution" (in the case of a DAF). The tax code imposes excise tax penalties on private foundations that make taxable expenditures and DAFs that make taxable distributions, as well as on foundation or DAF managers who knowingly approve a taxable expenditure or taxable distribution.

To avoid these excise taxes, as a private foundation or DAF grantor you generally must exercise ER in connection with any grant to an entity that is not recognized by the IRS as a public charity.

While that is the general rule, it is important we note at the outset that there are several exceptions. Specifically, DAFs may make grants to private operating, pass-through or common fund foundations (the latter two of which are rarely encountered entities) without exercising ER, and private foundations may make grants to exempt operating foundations (which also are rarely encountered) without exercising ER. Conversely, both DAFs and private foundations must exercise ER in connection with grants to certain supporting organizations (described in section 509(a)(3)), notably, Type III supporting organizations that are not "functionally integrated."[69]

In addition, as an alternative to exercising ER with respect to grants to some foreign organizations, as a private foundation or DAF grantor you may elect to make a determination that a foreign organization is the equivalent of a US public charity (an equivalency determination or ED), in which case ER will not be required. ED is discussed in more detail in **Chapter Six**. ER also is not required in connection with grants made to foreign governments, agencies or instrumentalities of foreign governments or international organizations designated by executive order

---

[69] *See* Code section 170(b)(1)(F), Code section 4945(d)(4)(A)(iii) and Code sections 4966(c)(2)(A) and 4945(d)(4)(A)(ii).

under 22 U.S.C. 288,[70] in each case so long as the grants are made exclusively for charitable purposes.

The Expenditure Responsibility Process

The ER process requires four basic steps (with a small difference in the fourth step for DAF grantors). Specifically, to exercise ER, as a private foundation or DAF grantor you must:

◆ Conduct a pre-grant inquiry;

◆ Make the grant pursuant to a written grant agreement;

◆ Require and receive reports from the grantee; and

◆ For private foundation grantors, report on Form 990-PF any grants for which ER is required.[71]

While the four steps to ER sound quite simple, as a private foundation or DAF grantor you should note that the Treasury Regulations contain specific instructions for how each step should be met. We will review each in turn.

Conducting a Pre-Grant Inquiry

As a private foundation or DAF grantor, you must conduct a pre-grant inquiry regarding a potential ER grantee. The scope of this inquiry can vary but, as a general matter, the inquiry should be complete enough to give a reasonable person assurance that the grantee will use the grant for its intended purposes.

A properly-completed pre-grant inquiry should record and document matters that speak to the grantee's ability to carry out the intended grant purposes properly. These matters include the identity, prior history, and experience of the grantee, its management, and those members of its staff who will be working on the activities funded by the grant. In addition, as the grantor, you also should document any knowledge you have of (based on prior experience or otherwise), or other information which is readily available concerning, the management, activities, and prac-

---

[70] A list of these international organizations appears as **Appendix A**.

[71] As of the date of this writing, the Form 990, filed by public charities such as DAFs, does not require reporting of grants for which expenditure responsibility is required, though it may in the future. As a general matter, we recommend that DAFs still maintain complete records for ER grants in the same manner as private foundations.

Sample Pre-Grant Inquiry Form

This is a suggested document with sample questions to better get to know your grantees. It should not be considered comprehensive.

Name of the proposed grantee:_____

When was the organization founded: _____

What are the primary purposes of the organization: _____
_____
_____

How is the organization classified/registered:_____
_____
_____

Names and titles of chief personnel of the proposed grantee, including a brief statement as to how their background and experience contribute to the intended purpose of the grant:_____
_____
_____

Summary of previous grants or other assistance (if any) made by [YOUR ORGANIZATION] to proposed grantee, including whether proper use of grants was made and whether required reports were filed with [YOUR ORGANIZATION]: _____
_____
_____

Summary of grants awarded by other foundations to the proposed grantee including the amount of the grant, date awarded and the purpose of the grant (comment on whether the proposed grantee has had a history of compliance or non-compliance with the terms of these grants): _____
_____
_____

Brief summary of knowledge of [YOUR ORGANIZATION], based on prior experience or other information readily available, concerning the prior history and experience of the proposed grantee and its chief personnel including grantee's activities and practices (or reference to specific documents in [YOUR ORGANIZATION'S] files covering these points):_____
_____
_____

Brief statement of basis for conclusion that the proposed grantee will use the grant for the proper purposes: _____
_____
_____

tices of the grantee. This can range from a simple online search of the grantee's name, to be sure that it does not appear in news articles documenting operational problems or other potential issues, to a scan of the grantee's name through a worldwide compliance database to check for money-laundering, sanctions-related, or terrorist-financing issues. As a private foundation or DAF grantor, you may also consider speaking with peer grantors about their experiences with a potential grantee, as those conversations may provide additional knowledge and information for your pre-grant inquiry file.

In conducting a pre-grant inquiry, and particularly in determining its scope, as a private foundation or DAF you may consider the size and purpose of the grant, the period over which it will be paid and whether your prior experience with the grantee provides comfort that the grantee has the capacity to use the grant funds for the intended charitable purposes. For example, a pre-grant inquiry in connection with a one-time payment, $1,500 grant to a grantee that a private foundation grantor has funded for years will be (appropriately) much more limited in scope than a pre-grant inquiry in connection with a multi-year $1.5 million grant to a grantee with which the private foundation has no direct prior experience. In either case, as the grantor, you should document and retain evidence of your pre-grant inquiry.

In addition to and in conjunction with your pre-grant inquiry, you as the grantor and the grantee should work together to define the intended charitable purpose of the grant carefully. Compliance with the technical steps of ER will be for naught if the purposes of the grant itself are not exclusively charitable. A well-defined grant purpose will set out clearly the problems intended to be addressed by the grant, the activities to be carried out by the grantee to address those problems, and how addressing those problems is consistent with the grantor's charitable mission.

Written Grant Agreements

Assuming that, after conducting a pre-grant inquiry, as a private foundation or DAF grantor you are satisfied that your potential grantee will be able to use the grant for its intended purposes, you must enter into a written grant agreement with the grantee. It is important to note that the Treasury Regulations provide very specific content requirements for written grant agreements, so grantors should take care to ensure that their agreements contain the required provisions and therefore meet the ER requirements.

As a first step, the written grant agreement should clearly specify the purposes of the grant in a manner that would allow a third party reviewing the agreement to understand what charitable activities the grantee will carry out with the grant funds. Since many grantors require specific and detailed grant proposals before considering making a grant to a grantee, we have found that referencing the portion of a grant proposal that describes the grantee's proposed activities in detail, and then attaching that portion as an exhibit, is an effective way to include a clear description of the grant purposes in a written grant agreement.

Next, the written grant agreement needs to include a commitment by the grantee:

- ◆ To repay any portion of the grant which is not used for the grant purposes;

- ◆ To submit full and complete reports (on at least an annual basis) on the manner in which the funds are spent and the progress made in accomplishing the grant purposes;

- ◆ To maintain records of receipts and expenditures and to make its books and records available to the grantor at reasonable times; and

- ◆ Not to use any of the grant funds:

  - ❖ To attempt to influence legislation (though see our note later on);

  - ❖ To influence the outcome of any specific public election, or to carry on, directly or indirectly, any voter registration drive;

  - ❖ To make subsequent grants to other organizations, unless the grantee also exercises ER with respect to those grants;

  - ❖ To make grants to individuals; or

  - ❖ To undertake any activity that is not in furtherance of charitable purposes.[72]

Many private foundation and DAF grantors find it convenient to use a template grant agreement for all of their ER grants which contains each of the above-described commitments. This helps ensure that none of

---

[72] *See* Treasury Regulations section 53.4945-5(b)(3).

the commitments are missed with respect to a particular grantee and is helpful in maintaining clear and consistent ER files.

Finally, the written grant agreement must be signed by an appropriate officer, director or trustee of the grantee. This typically will be an executive officer of the grantee, with signatory authority, who is familiar with the intended purposes of the grant.

Overcoming Challenges Relating to Written Grant Agreements

As the section above makes clear, a properly drafted written grant agreement places significant restrictions on a grantee's ability to utilize grant funds. This is intentional; when the ER rules were drafted, Congress wished to protect against the use of private foundation dollars for noncharitable purposes. However noble their intentions, though, the restrictions can make it challenging for a private foundation or DAF grantor to accomplish the charitable goals of particular grants.

Subgrants

For example, a written grant agreement must contain a provision restricting a grantee from making subsequent grants from grant funds to other organizations that are not public charities unless the grantee exercises ER with respect to the subsequent grants. Many organizations, particularly outside the United States, may work with and fund other organizations to accomplish their charitable goals, and so are implicated by this rule. For a foreign grantee that is not familiar with the ER requirements, this can be confusing. For a grantor, the idea of tracking whether its grantee is properly exercising ER over a subsequent grantee can be intimidating.

Helpfully, we do have some indication from the IRS—albeit nonprecedential—as to how it expects a grantor to monitor its ER grantees when subsequent grants may be part of the grantee's charitable activities. The IRS has ruled that an original grantor satisfied its ER obligations by binding its grantee, via a written grant agreement, to exercise ER with respect to subsequent grants to other organizations that were not public charities. The IRS did not hold the grantor responsible for the grantee's exercise of ER; rather, the grantor was held responsible only for actions within its control.[73]

---

[73] *See* Private Letter Ruling 9717024 (April 25, 1998). While private letter rulings are not precedential authority, they are useful indicators of the IRS's thinking on particular points.

Lobbying

As stated above, a written grant agreement must contain a provision prohibiting the grantee from using any of the grant funds to influence legislation (i.e., to engage in lobbying). This restriction makes reasonable sense in the context of private foundation grantors—after all, private foundations are not permitted to lobby or to expend funds in support of lobbying activities. DAFs, however, are public charities and therefore are not subject to a prohibition on lobbying. For example, a public charity can engage in, or support, insubstantial lobbying activities. Why should this be different for a DAF making an ER grant?

Unfortunately, neither the IRS nor the Department of the Treasury has issued clear guidance as to whether DAFs may permit ER grantees to engage in insubstantial lobbying activities. Accordingly, until there is clear guidance one way or the other, we believe that the issue is sufficiently uncertain that we advise you as a DAF grantor to continue to prohibit lobbying in your ER grant agreements.

Reporting

The next step in the ER process is ensuring that an ER grantee provides regular and appropriately detailed reports regarding its use of grant funds. At a minimum, ER grantees must provide reports to grantors each year until the grant funds are expended in full, or the grant is otherwise terminated. Annual reports must be submitted to grantors within a reasonable period of time after the end of the annual accounting period (i.e., the fiscal year) of the grantee to which the report refers.

Reports must include: (i) a description of the grantee's use of the grant funds over the reporting period; (ii) confirmation that the grantee has complied with the terms of the written grant agreement; and (iii) a report on the progress made by the grantee in achieving the purposes for which the grant was made.

In our experience, many private foundation and DAF grantors find the reporting requirements to be the most onerous of the ER requirements. Grantees—particularly smaller grantees—may be slow to complete reports or may not automatically include the information that the ER rules require. One trick to easing the reporting burden for grantees— and therefore making compliance with the ER rules easier for you as a grantor—is to make the reporting *process* as simple as possible. For example, you may consider providing a template report to your grantees with the written ER grant agreement, so that the grantee need only fill in the relevant data and return the report. We also are increasingly seeing grantors provide grantees with the ability to submit reports online through a website, which both gives grantors the ability to control the form and content of the report and makes completion and submission simpler for grantees.

Overcoming Reporting-Related Challenges

To comply with the ER rules, as a private foundation or DAF grantor, you must require reports from your grantee until the grant funds are extinguished in full. So, how should you handle reporting if you wish to make a grant to fund an endowment, where the grant funds may never be extinguished in full, or to purchase capital equipment or fund other capital projects, where (for example) the purchased equipment may have a long useful life? The short answer is—it depends on the identity of the grantee!

The Treasury Regulations provide that if a private foundation grantor makes an ER grant to an *IRS-recognized private foundation* for endowment, for the purchase of capital equipment, or for other capital purposes, the grantee must provide annual reports for the year in which the grant was made and the immediately succeeding two years, for a total of three years. If the grantor is satisfied that the grant is being used for proper purposes at the end of this period, the grantee need not submit further reports. However, this exception exists only for grants to IRS-recognized private foundations. For grants to other organizations, such as foreign organizations that do not have IRS determination letters, endowment and capital equipment grants create difficult (and potentially perpetual) reporting burdens.

As a general matter, many private foundation and DAF grantors that make ER grants for capital equipment elect to require reports for the "useful life" of the equipment, using generally accepted accounting principles and current US law regarding the depreciation of equipment. This approach has been endorsed by the Council on Foundations and continues to be fairly common in the field.[74] Practitioners have called for

---

[74] John A. Edie and Jane C. Nober, *Beyond Our Borders: A Guide to Making Grants Outside the United States, 3rd ed.* (Council on Foundations, Inc., 2002), pages 34-35.

the IRS to amend the reporting rules or provide clarifying guidance but, as of this writing, no such amendments or guidance have been issued.[75]

The "Separate Account" Requirement

Another issue of controversy and confusion in the ER context is a provision in the Treasury Regulations that states a private foundation or DAF grantor to an ER grantee can be "reasonably assured" that its grant funds will be used exclusively for charitable purposes only if the grantee agrees to continuously maintain the grant funds in a separate fund dedicated to charitable purposes.[76] Does this mean that as grantor you must require your grantee to open a separate bank account for the grant funds?

Practically, some foreign organizations are not permitted by local law to maintain more than one bank account, so such a requirement would be highly problematic. Fortunately, the IRS is aware of this issue and, while it has not issued formal guidance on this point, we believe that a grantee can comply with the "separate fund" requirement so long as it can account separately for the grant funds instead of holding the funds in a separate account. Of course, to the extent that a grantee can maintain funds in a separate account, doing so may help to ease its reporting obligations.

Maintaining Records: How Grantors Can Comply with Retention and Reporting Requirements

The last step in the ER process is the maintenance of records by the grantor and—for private foundation grantors—accurate and timely reporting of ER grants on Form 990-PF.

The Treasury Regulations provide fairly straightforward record retention requirements for grantors. Grantors must maintain, at their principal office, the following documentation:

◆ A copy of each written grant agreement with an ER grantee;

◆ A copy of each report received from each ER grantee; and

---

[75] As we discuss in the next chapter, a grantor seeking to make an endowment or other capital purpose grant is well-advised to consider making an ED with respect to its proposed grantee as an alternative to making an ER grant.

[76] *See* Treasury Regulations section 53.4945-5(c)(3)(ii); Treasury Regulations section 53.4945-6(c).

◆ A copy of each report made by the grantor's employees or independent auditors of any audits or other investigations made with respect to any ER grants.[77]

The Treasury Regulations generally speak to retention of current records (i.e., grant agreements, grantee reports and internal reports for the *current year*), and as a grantor you must make those documents available to the IRS upon request. However, as a general matter, most grantors elect to maintain their ER files for multiyear periods in accordance with their standard document retention policies and practices. To the extent that as a grantor you maintain your files electronically, your ER files should be clearly labeled and categorized such that grant agreements and reports for each ER grantee can be located easily.

In addition to maintaining records, private foundation grantors must report their ER grants annually on Form 990-PF. As a private foundation grantor, you will need to indicate on Line 5c of Part VII-B of the Form 990-PF if you exercised ER in connection with a grant over the relevant tax year. You also will need to attach a statement listing your ER grants and including the following information:

◆ The name and address of the grantee;

◆ The date and amount of the grant;

◆ The grant purpose;

◆ The amount of the grant expended by the grantee as of the date of the most recent grantee report;

◆ Whether, to your knowledge, the grantee has diverted any portion of the grant from the grant purpose;

◆ The dates of any reports received from the grantee; and

◆ The dates and results of any audit or other verification of the grantee's report by you.[78]

As mentioned previously, the Form 990, which is the information return filed by public charities, currently does not require reporting on ER grants by DAFs (i.e., the only public charities that need exercise ER).

---

[77] *See* Treasury Regulations section 53.4945-5(d)(3).
[78] *See* Treasury Regulations section 53-4945-5(d)(2).

Notwithstanding the lack of a reporting mechanism on the Form 990, DAFs are well advised to maintain records in the manner described above with respect to their ER grants.

How to Address a Violation of the ER Requirements?

No matter how carefully a private foundation or DAF grantor structures its ER grants, there is always the possibility that a grantee, intentionally or, more frequently, unintentionally, will take (or fail to take) an action that will result in a violation of the ER requirements.

Most frequently, as alluded to above, this happens in the context of reporting. A grantor will enter into a multi-year expenditure responsibility grant but, after year one, the grantee will cease providing timely reports. So what is a grantor to do? The Treasury Regulations require that, first, as the grantor, you make a reasonable effort to obtain the required report. This can include emailing or telephoning the grantee or, if you make site visits, reminding the grantee in person that it is not fulfilling its reporting requirements. In addition, the Treasury Regulations require that you withhold all future payments on your current grant *and any other grants to the same grantee* until the report has been received. While grantors typically are loathe to withhold funding from important charitable projects, it is both required by the Treasury Regulations and likely to incentivize the grantee to get its act together and furnish the missing report.

Less frequently, though of more concern, a grantor will determine that one of its ER grantees has used grant funds for improper purposes. In such a circumstance, the Treasury Regulations provide that as a grantor you must take "all reasonable and appropriate steps" either to recover the grant funds, or to ensure the restoration of the diverted funds to the proper purpose and the dedication of other grant funds provided to the grantee to proper purposes. The Treasury Regulations provide that "all reasonable and appropriate steps" includes legal action, where appropriate, but that legal action is not required if, in all probability, it would not result in the recovery of the grant funds.[79] We note this not to suggest that you immediately should threaten legal action in the event that grant funds appear to have been diverted from their intended purposes but to highlight how seriously the IRS and Treasury view diversions of charitable funds. Regardless of the specific actions you take to recover

---

[79] *See* Treasury Regulations section 53.4945-5(e)(1)(v).

or restore diverted funds, you also must withhold any further payments to the grantee until you have both received assurances from the grantee that future diversions will not occur and required the grantee to take extraordinary precautions to prevent future diversions from occurring.

These can be difficult conversations for a grantor, but the Treasury Regulations do not permit grantors simply to abandon diverted grant funds. The grantor need not be successful in recovering or restoring diverted funds, but grantors must at least make a reasonable effort to do so.

While, at first glance, the ER process may seem complex and onerous, a well-advised and well-organized private foundation or DAF grantor generally should find the process both workable and not significantly different from its standard grant process. For organizations that make numerous ER grants, developing standard procedures and templates will help to ease the process administratively and often will assist grantors in maintaining their compliance.

John Bennett

John Bennett is an Associate at Simpson Thacher & Bartlett LLP where he practices in the Exempt Organizations Group. He advises a variety of international and domestic exempt organizations, including all forms of private foundations and public charities, on structural and operating issues such as formation, governance, reorganizations, domestic and international grantmaking, and taxation.

John also advises endowed public charities and private foundations in connection with investment-related matters, including with respect to traditional private fund and managed account investments as well as impact investments and mission- and program-related investments. In addition, John is a regular speaker on topics of interest to exempt organizations.

John earned his JD at Columbia Law School, where he was a James Kent Scholar and a Harlan Fiske Stone Scholar, and earned his BA degree from Tufts University.

David Shevlin

David Shevlin is a Partner at Simpson Thacher & Bartlett LLP and is head of the Exempt Organizations Group. He advises a variety of international and domestic exempt organizations, including all forms of private foundations and public charities. David also advises donors to and the governing bodies of exempt organizations.

David has been recognized as a leading not-for-profit lawyer in *The Legal 500 United States* (2013) and as a leading practitioner in *Chambers USA: America's Leading Lawyers for Business* (2008–2013). In addition, he regularly speaks and writes on topics of relevance to exempt organizations.

David earned his JD, *magna cum laude*, at New York University where he was named a member of Order of the Coif, and earned his BS degree from Cornell University, where he was named a Presidential Scholar.

Chapter Six

Tools for Direct International Grantmaking: Equivalency Determination

David Shevlin and John Bennett

As we discussed in **Chapter Five**, certain grants by private foundations, as well as certain grants by sponsoring organizations of donor advised funds (DAFs)[80] require the private foundation or DAF grantor to exercise expenditure responsibility (ER) to avoid the imposition of excise taxes in respect of such grants. As we mentioned in **Chapter Five**, as an alternative to ER with respect to grants to some foreign organizations, private foundation and DAF grantors may elect to make *a good faith determination* that a foreign organization is the equivalent of a US public charity (an equivalency determination or ED), in which case ER will not be required.[81]

Like the ER rules, the ED rules set forth a specific and detailed process for private foundation and DAF grantors to follow before a grant is made, but the ED rules provide private foundation and DAF grantors with somewhat more flexibility than ER. In particular, private foundation and DAF grantors may find ED to be a more attractive option than ER when contemplating making grants in support of an endowment fund or for

---

[80] While it is the sponsoring organization of a DAF that makes each DAF grant, we use the vernacular term *donor advised fund* (DAF) in this chapter to refer to sponsoring organizations.

[81] As a reminder, private foundation and DAF grantors may make grants to foreign governments, agencies or international organizations designated by Executive Order under 22 U.S.C. 288 without exercising ER or making an ED, so long as the grants are made exclusively for charitable purposes.

the purchase of capital equipment, or where a grant may involve sub-grants to other foreign organizations.

This chapter describes the circumstances in which an ED may be used as an alternative to exercising ER, walks through each step of the ED process in detail and provides practical tips for you as a private foundation or DAF grantor to consider when preparing to make an ED in connection with a grant.

When Can a Grantor Make an Equivalency Determination?

As discussed in **Chapter Five**, a grant by a private foundation or a DAF to an organization that is not recognized by the IRS as a public charity will be deemed a "taxable expenditure" (in the case of a private foundation) or a "taxable distribution" (in the case of a DAF). The tax code imposes excise tax penalties on private foundations that make taxable expenditures and DAFs that make taxable distributions, as well as on foundation or DAF managers who knowingly approve a taxable expenditure or taxable distribution.

Private foundation and DAF grantors generally may avoid these excise taxes by exercising ER in connection with any grant to an entity that is not recognized by the IRS as a public charity. As an alternative to the ER process, private foundation and DAF grantors considering a grant to a foreign organization may consider making an ED.[82] A private foundation grantor that makes an ED in connection with a grant to a foreign organization also may count the grant as a qualifying distribution for purposes of meeting its annual distribution requirements.[83]

While private foundations have long utilized the ED process for grants to foreign organizations, before 2015 there was no clear guidance from the IRS that DAF grantors also could make EDs as an alternative to exercising ER. Since, as a practical matter, many DAFs already were making EDs in connection with foreign grants, the sector was pleased to see confir-

---

[82] Grantors may not utilize the ED process for grants to US organizations that are not public charities.

[83] A detailed discussion is outside the scope of this chapter, but section 4942 of the Internal Revenue Code of 1986, as amended (the Code), requires that private foundations distribute a certain amount of income in each year in the form of qualifying distributions or be subject to excise taxes. As a general matter, qualifying distributions, defined in Code section 4942(g), are those distributions made in furtherance of a private foundation's charitable purposes.

mation in final Treasury Regulations issued on September 25, 2015 (the "Final Regulations") that DAFs also may make EDs.[84]

The Equivalency Determination Process[85]

Before 2012, the ED process had been unchanged for many years and was described in the Treasury Regulations and in Revenue Procedure 92-94 (Rev. Proc. 92-94), which provided a simplified procedure for private foundations to follow in making EDs. In 2012, the IRS and the Department of the Treasury published proposed regulations updating the ED process and, in 2015, the Final Regulations amended and finalized those proposed regulations. Then, on September 14, 2017, the IRS published Revenue Procedure 2017-53 (Rev. Proc. 2017-53) which provides specific guidelines for making EDs under the terms of the Final Regulations.

> The Final Regulations do not set out separate ED procedures for DAFs but rather provide that DAFs may rely on the ED procedures for private foundations until further guidance is issued. As of the time of this writing, further guidance specific to DAFs has not yet been issued, and DAFs may continue to rely on the Final Regulations for ED procedures.

Written Advice or In-House EDs

The Final Regulations provide that a private foundation or DAF grantor may make a "good faith determination" that a foreign organization which has not been classified by the IRS as a US public charity or private operating foundation is the equivalent of a US public charity and, therefore, that a grant to that foreign organization will be treated as a grant made to a US public charity. Your determination that a foreign organization is the equivalent of a US public charity ordinarily will be considered a "good faith" determination if it is based on the written advice of a qualified tax practitioner. For purposes of the Final Regulations, a qualified tax prac-

---

[84] *See* Federal Register at 80 FR 57709.
[85] This chapter describes the ED process as it relates to typical *public* charities (e.g., schools, churches, hospitals, publicly-supported organizations, etc.). Additional requirements apply in connection with the ED process for foreign organizations that may be equivalent to US private operating foundations, exempt operating foundations and non-functionally integrated Type III supporting organizations, for example, and grantors generally should seek additional guidance in those circumstances.

titioner is an attorney, a certified public accountant or an enrolled agent who is licensed in a state, territory or possession of the United States (or, for enrolled agents, enrolled by the IRS).[86]

It is important to note that private foundation and DAF grantors are permitted to make EDs without relying on the written advice of a qualified tax practitioner. Rather, reliance on the written advice of a qualified tax practitioner allows private foundation and DAF grantors to take advantage of the "special rule," as the IRS describes it, providing that an ED ordinarily will be considered made in good faith if it is based on current written advice from a qualified tax practitioner.

A private foundation or DAF grantor still may make an ED without advice from a qualified tax practitioner, relying on the "general rule" that a grant to a foreign organization where the grantor has made a good faith determination that the foreign organization is the equivalent of a US public charity will not be a taxable expenditure (for a private foundation) or a taxable distribution (for a DAF) and will be a qualifying distribution (for a private foundation), the distinction being that the determination *will not automatically be considered to be made in good faith*. Accordingly, if your private foundation or DAF makes EDs without relying on written advice, you should ensure that (i) the staff responsible for making the EDs have an understanding of US charity tax law, (ii) the staff are basing their EDs on affidavits of foreign organization grantees that include all of the information we describe below as required in connection with written advice and (iii) the staff is documenting all of its ED procedures and maintaining all relevant documentation.

An alternative for cost-conscious private foundation or DAF grantors that may not want to engage a qualified tax practitioner to provide written advice in connection with an ED, but that may not have staff with appropriate experience with US charity tax law and the ED process to make EDs in house, is a so-called ED "repository." These organizations, some of which offer tiered annual membership costs and some of which will provide EDs without a membership requirement, work with a number of private foundation and DAF grantors and maintain a database of previously-completed EDs so that, when a grantor seeks an ED for a foreign organization, the repository may be able to provide written advice from a qualified tax practitioner in its employ at a lower cost as it already will have completed the required diligence on the foreign organization.

---

[86] Note that this means a private foundation or DAF grantor may not rely on advice from non-US counsel in making an ED.

The ED Process: What Do We Need to Obtain?

As noted above, Rev. Proc. 2017-53 outlines the guidelines that a qualified tax practitioner should use in preparing written advice for a private foundation or DAF grantor making an ED in connection with a grant to a foreign organization. It also describes the documentation that the qualified tax practitioner should obtain to demonstrate the basis for the written advice. As a general matter, a qualified tax practitioner's written advice should contain enough factual detail about the foreign organization's operations and support to enable the IRS to determine that the foreign organization likely would qualify as a US public charity. Rev. Proc. 2017-53 explains that the factual detail in "preferred written advice" (i.e., advice that meets the guidelines set forth in Rev. Proc. 2017-53) may be based on affidavits received from the foreign organization (and signed by an officer or trustee of the foreign organization with knowledge of the relevant facts), as well as a review of the foreign organization's governing documents and the laws applicable to the foreign organization.[87]

Organizational Documents—Purposes, Dissolution Clauses, Inurement, and Lobbying

A qualified tax practitioner preparing written advice to make an ED is, in effect, gathering the material that would be required to be provided to the IRS with Form 1023 in connection with a US organization's application for recognition as a public charity.[88] Instead of the IRS determining the foreign organization is a public charity, however, you, the private foundation or DAF grantor, stand in the shoes of the IRS and make that determination with respect to the foreign organization. Accordingly, and pursuant to the procedures of Rev. Proc. 2017-53, your qualified tax practitioner should obtain copies of the foreign organization's governing documents (e.g., certificate of incorporation, bylaws, etc.), translated into English if not originally written in English. The foreign organization's governing documents should confirm that:

◆ The foreign organization is organized exclusively for charitable purposes (as defined under Code section 501(c)(3));

---

[87] *See* Rev. Proc. 2017-53, Sec. 4.01. A qualified tax practitioner is permitted to rely on English translations of documents originally not written in English or translations of foreign laws.
[88] The Form 1023 Application for Recognition of Exemption Under Section 501(c)(3) of the Internal Revenue Code is the form filed with the IRS to request recognition of charitable status.

◆ If the foreign organization were to dissolve, then all of its assets will be distributed to another nonprofit organization for charitable purposes or to a governmental entity for public use;

◆ The foreign organization does not have any shareholders or members with an ownership interest in the organization's income or assets, and the foreign organization does not distribute its income or assets other than for charitable purposes, to pay reasonable compensation, or to pay for property purchased at fair market value; and

◆ The foreign organization engages in no more than insubstantial lobbying activities and does not engage in political campaign activities.

Each of these four points is required of US public charities and, if a US organization applying for public charity status is unable to point to a provision in its governing documents (or in state law) that puts into place each one of the restrictions, the IRS will not approve its application.

Of course, the laws applicable to foreign organizations will differ from US law and, if any of the required points are *not* contained in the foreign organization's governing documents, then the qualified tax practitioner should confirm whether the requirement is provided for under law in the country in which the foreign organization is organized. For example, a foreign organization's governing documents may not need to provide that, at dissolution, its assets will be distributed only for charitable purposes, *if* there is a requirement under local law that *all* organizations of that type may upon dissolution distribute assets only for charitable purposes. This is similar to the question on Form 1023, for example, that asks if a US organization's governing documents contain a similar dissolution provision or if the organization relies on state law. In either case, the written advice should reference the relevant provisions and attach the governing documents and/or applicable foreign law. Finally, a qualified tax practitioner's written advice should refer to and describe any organization that controls the foreign organization, or that is operated in connection with the foreign organization.

The Narrative

Written advice also should describe the foreign organization's past, current and anticipated activities, including how the foreign organization funds and carries out its activities. You can think of this section of the written advice as similar to the narrative section of the Form 1023, in which the US organization describes to the IRS what it will do that qualifies it as a public charity. In fact, a qualified tax practitioner may use schedules from the Form 1023 or the Form 990 (an IRS-recognized public charity's annual information return) to demonstrate information regarding a foreign organization's

For private foundation and DAF grantors who will make EDs in-house, without receiving written advice, familiarity with US tax law is especially important for this part of an ED, as the grantor's records should demonstrate that staff reviewed the foreign organization's purposes and activities and determined that the organization operates exclusively for charitable purposes.

charitable activities or revenue streams.[89] This section also should reference the basis of the information it describes (i.e., whether it came from an affidavit from the foreign organization or other sources). Finally, the written advice should apply US tax law to the facts to determine whether the foreign organization is operated exclusively for charitable purposes. Again, this is in large part the same analysis that a qualified tax practitioner would undertake in drafting a Form 1023 for a US public charity.

Public Support: Challenges and Tips

Just as there are many ways for a US organization to be classified as a public charity, a foreign organization can demonstrate its equivalence to a US public charity in a number of ways. A foreign organization may be the equivalent of a public charity based on its status as a church, or based on its status as an educational institution or because it raises funds from members of the general public and therefore is "publicly supported."[90] Determining that a foreign organization is the equivalent of a publicly supported US public charity can present particular challenges. Specifically, a qualified tax practitioner's written advice with respect to a publicly supported foreign organization must include a schedule of financial information that demonstrates that the foreign organization meets *the public support test* applicable to US public charities.

---

[89] *See* Sec. 5.08 of Rev. Proc. 2017-53.
[90] *See* Code section 170(b)(1)(A)(i), Code section 170(b)(1)(A)(ii) and Code section 170(b)(1)(A)(vi), respectively.

For a foreign organization that has been in existence for more than five years (i.e., an organization that would have to demonstrate its public support to the IRS, if it was a US public charity), the organization can complete Schedule A to the Form 990, which is where a US public charity demonstrates public support. The completed Schedule A, demonstrating that the organization meets the public support test, should be appended to, and referenced in, the written advice. The challenge for many foreign organizations, however, is that they may not maintain their books and records in a manner that makes separating out and listing the information required on Schedule A easy to do. For example, a foreign organization may not be able to easily ascertain which of its donors provided more than 2 percent of the total support the organization received over the previous five years (whose contributions therefore need to be limited for purposes of the public support test). In such cases, the foreign organization will need to complete Schedule A to the best of its ability and the qualified tax practitioner will have to determine if the information provided is definitive enough to serve as the basis for written advice.

Helpfully, Rev. Proc. 2017-53 provides three positive clarifications for private foundation and DAF grantors making EDs. First, Rev. Proc. 2017-53 clarifies that, if a foreign organization has been in existence for less than five years, a qualified tax practitioner's written advice need only determine that the foreign organization can reasonably be expected to be publicly supported over the first five years of its existence. This is consistent with how the IRS makes determinations with respect to newly-formed US public charities. Second, Rev. Proc. 2017-53 confirms that all of a foreign organization's support from domestic or foreign charitable organizations qualifies as public support. Prior to the issuance of Rev. Proc. 2017-53, whether only domestic or both foreign and domestic support from other charitable organizations could be included as public support was not clear. Finally, Rev. Proc. 2017-53 confirms that, *for purposes of making EDs only*, all support from a domestic government, from a foreign government, or from an international organization designated by executive order under 22 U.S.C. 288 counts in full as public support. This previously had been a matter of debate, as the IRS had issued conflicting guidance in the form of a Revenue Ruling and two General Counsel Memorandums in the late 1970s and early 1980s,[91] and the clarification is very helpful in the ED context as many foreign organizations receive significant support from governments or governmental agencies and international organizations.

---

[91] *See* Revenue Ruling 75-435, G.C.M. 37001 and G.C.M. 38327.

Foreign Schools and Nondiscriminatory Policies

Another complex issue relates to EDs in the context of foreign schools. In the 1970s, because of concerns that US private schools were discriminating on the basis of race and because the information and representations the IRS required from private schools often was not sufficient for making a determination as to whether the schools were engaging in racial discrimination, the IRS issued two revenue rulings. Revenue Ruling 71-447 ("Rev. Proc. 71-447"), the first of the two, requires any school that wishes to be exempt under section 501(c)(3) to have implemented a racially nondiscriminatory policy. The second, Revenue Ruling 75-50 ("Rev. Proc. 75-50"), requires a school to include a statement in its governing documents (or in a resolution of its governing body) that it has a racially nondiscriminatory policy as to students and does not discriminate on the basis of race, color, and national or ethnic origin.[92]

Rev. Proc. 92-94, the predecessor to Rev. Proc. 2017-53 described above, required foreign schools to demonstrate compliance with Rev. Proc. 75-50, which proved difficult for foreign schools for a myriad of reasons. Rev. Proc. 2017-53 acknowledges that strict compliance with Rev. Proc. 75-50 may be impracticable in foreign countries and relaxes the procedures set forth in Rev. Rul. 92-94 somewhat. However, a qualified tax practitioner making an ED in respect of a foreign school still must:

◆ Confirm in written advice (or attach an affidavit confirming) that the foreign school has adopted a racially nondiscriminatory policy in its governing documents (or in a resolution of its governing body), and

◆ Provide evidence in written advice (or in an attached affidavit) that the foreign school actually operates in a racially nondiscriminatory manner.

A qualified tax practitioner preparing a written advice can use Rev. Proc. 75-50 as a guide for the type of evidence that demonstrates a foreign school operates in a racially nondiscriminatory manner, but strict compliance with Rev. Proc. 75-50 is not required.

---

[92] The school also must include a statement of its racially nondiscriminatory policy in all brochures and catalogues dealing with student admission, programs and scholarships and must reference the racially nondiscriminatory policy in other written advertising that it uses as a means of informing prospective students of its programs.

If your private foundation or DAF is considering making a grant to a foreign school and the foreign school does not operate pursuant to a racially nondiscriminatory policy, you might consider working with the foreign school to draft a simple racially nondiscriminatory policy for adoption by its governing body. In fact, as a general matter, if you find that a foreign organization's governing documents are missing provisions that are required (or even simply helpful) in connection with an ED, we have found that foreign organizations often are willing to work with grantors to amend their governing documents to incorporate language that will make the ED process easier, both for you and for future private foundation or DAF grantors.

Documentation, Record Keeping, and Reporting

Although private foundation and DAF grantors making EDs in connection with grants to foreign organizations are not subject to the strict ER requirements as to documentation of grants, well-advised private foundation and DAF grantors often look to the ER rules for guidance in documenting ED grants. In particular, any time you make a grant to a foreign organization, even if using ED, we recommend entering into a written agreement with the foreign organization grantee that sets out explicitly the charitable purposes of the grant and the permitted uses of the grant funds. The written agreement can be simple, for a small grant, but many grantors will use written agreements similar to those used with ER grantees for larger or more complex grants.

In addition to a written grant agreement, private foundation and DAF grantors making EDs should maintain a grant file in connection with each ED, containing (i) the written advice received from a qualified tax practitioner (if written advice is obtained), (ii) all supporting documentation for the ED (e.g., the grantee affidavits, copies of governing documents and relevant foreign law) and (iii) the written grant agreement, if one is used.[93] Unlike ER grants, ED grants do not need to be separately reported on a private foundation's Form 990-PF or on a DAF's Form 990.

---

[93] Note that preferred written advice, for purposes of Rev. Proc. 2017-53, also should include confirmation that a foreign organization has not been designated or individually identified as a terrorist organization by the US government. *See* Sec. 5.09 of Rev. Proc. 20117-53. Evidence of this confirmation, as well as the result of any OFAC or other watch-list screenings (described in **Chapters Seven** and **Eight**) also should be retained in the ED file.

Currently Qualified Written Advice

A common question from private foundation and DAF grantors making EDs in connection with grants to foreign organizations is how often an ED must be updated (i.e., how often must you receive updated written advice or, if making an ED in-house, update your own ED files?). Generally, written advice will be current (so long as the relevant law on which the advice is based does not change) if the facts on which it is based are from the foreign organization's current or prior tax year. Accordingly, written advice still will be *current* for up to two years after the information on which it is based is provided.[94] For a foreign organization that has to demonstrate public support (as discussed above), written advice will remain current for two years following the end of the five-year period over which the grantee's public support was tested and demonstrated.[95] These time periods apply similarly for EDs made in-house—meaning you should reconfirm the information on which your ED is based and (as necessary) obtain updated support schedules at least every two years.

> As a matter of general practice, if a private foundation or DAF grantor becomes aware that the information on which an ED is based has changed and is no longer accurate, the grantor should no longer consider the ED as currently qualified.

ER and ED. Which Is Better When?

As you can see from the detail provided above, EDs can require more time and expense than ER for a private foundation or DAF grantor *before a grant is made*, but ER may involve more significant reporting burdens *over the grant period*. EDs may be particularly beneficial to private foundation and DAF grantors if: (i) you plan to establish a long-term relationship with the grantee (and thus will be making many grants), (ii) you want to make a grant to an endowment fund or to purchase capital equipment, (iii) you want to make a grant that involves subgrants to other foreign organizations, or (iv) you want to make a grant without explicitly prohibiting the use of grant funds for lobbying.

---

[94] Rev. Proc. 2017-53 provides an example of written advice issued in January 2017, based on information from January 2017, which would be "current" until December 2018 (assuming no change in the underlying laws).

[95] This generally matches the period of time for which grantors to US publicly supported charities may consider those charities publicly supported without seeking confirmation of continued public support.

As you will recall from **Chapter Five**, ER grants to fund endowments, purchase capital equipment, or to fund projects that involve subgrants, can be burdensome both to you and to your grantees. Endowment and capital equipment ER grants can require long-term (or event perpetual) reporting obligations, and grants involving subgrants can require the foreign organization to exercise ER concerning its own foreign organization grantees. Because an ED permits you to treat a grant to a foreign organization as you would treat a grant to a US public charity, these restrictions do not apply.[96] Also, you can make general support grants to foreign organizations using an ED, and therefore your grant agreement does not need to explicitly prohibit lobbying (though, of course, private foundations may not use the ED process to make grants for prohibited lobbying purposes). Finally, ED grantees do not need to maintain grant funds in a separate account or otherwise account separately on their books for grant funds. These features of ED can make the post-grant process more streamlined and less administratively burdensome, both for you and for your grantees.

On the other hand, if you are planning a one-time grant to a foreign organization, or even a multi-year grant that does not involve endowment or capital equipment purposes, the up-front costs of obtaining an ED (e.g., obtaining written advice from a qualified tax practitioner and/or staff time devoted to obtaining all of the necessary documentation on which to base an ED) may outweigh the later administrative convenience, such that exercising ER may be simplest.

In either case, remember that record keeping and close attention to the rules is critical to ensure that your organization is protected, and remember that you may (and probably will!) encounter roadblocks in the process for both ER and ED. Foreign grantmaking can be challenging, but there are many good resources available (including this book!) to guide you through the process.

***

David Shevlin and John Bennett

See author bios in **Chapter Five**.

***

---

[96] That being said, we recommend that, particularly in connection with grants to foreign organizations, grantors always confirm the identity of subgrantees before permitting subgrants.

Chapter Seven

Vetting International Charities

Jessie Krafft

The process of getting to know and trust a grantee that is thousands of miles away and operates in foreign legal context and languages can be truly daunting. Making international grants comes with many unique challenges that must be navigated artfully to make safe, effective, and compliant grants that follow your standards and philanthropic strategies. To do this efficiently, it is essential that you develop a replicable, risk-based vetting process that holds your grantees to certain standards while remaining flexible to any curveballs that may fly your way.

Vetting international charities requires creativity, empathy, and great attention to detail. Is it even possible to build all of that into a vetting checklist?! It *is* possible, but it must be done cautiously. The *checklist approach* can easily lead to a process that doesn't ask questions tailored to unique circumstances. You must encourage your process to move beyond the checklist and toward a flexible, *risk-based approach*.

This chapter will help guide you through various aspects you should consider in developing your organization's vetting process. But it won't do the work for you! The process must be customized to consider a variety of things: organizational-risk appetite, philanthropic strategy, vetting the grant purpose and program itself, the type of partners you want your grantees to be, and the locations of your grantees (to name a few factors). This chapter will guide you through some best practices and will equip you to develop an effective and flexible vetting process.

How to Develop a Risk-Based Approach to Vetting International Charities

We love the IRS! Okay, more context needed, I know. As international grantmakers from the United States, we have the choice of using either equivalency determination (ED) or expenditure responsibility (ER) to make grants to organizations that are not 501(c)(3) charitable entities. I use the word *organizations*, and not *nonprofits* or *charities*, very consciously. With these tools, we are able to make grants to many different types of organizations; they do not necessarily need to be charitable entities or even nonprofits. However, there is a baseline requirement that the organization must be able to undertake (and that you are funding) a project with an "exempt" or "charitable" purpose, as defined by the IRS. I will not go into a lot of detail about the distinction between ER and ED, as this was covered masterfully by **Chapters Five** and **Six**.

Utilizing both of these tools requires more staff training and process development, but the ability to seamlessly switch between the two as needed will allow you to have a lot more choice in your grantee partners and the types of projects that you fund. Some foreign organizations just cannot meet the strict requirements of ED without changing their bylaws or modifying their practices, but that doesn't necessarily mean that they're not a suitable grantee. ER, on the other hand, allows you the possibility of working with these organizations. If your board of directors and your vetting process allow you to choose between the two, it is important to set clear parameters for when you would use which. The table below provides a brief (though not comprehensive) overview of grantee and project characteristics that could steer you toward ER or ED in your vetting process. A close reading of **Chapters Five** and **Six** will help you understand the reasoning behind some of these choices, and it will help you understand how to structure your vetting process around those IRS protocols.

Regardless of the tool that you choose, many parts of the vetting process should remain the same. It often comes down to a question of how flexible you can be, as ED is more stringent in many ways. For example, we consider it to be a best practice to read and understand the governing documents of an organization with both ED and ER. If the organization is empowered by their documents to undertake some activities that are not considered "exempt purposes," this would likely be a deal-breaker for ED, while it may simply be a red flag under ER. You may just need to ask more questions if it concerns you that some of their activities are not charitable or to ensure that your funds would not be expended on those activities. This example illustrates one factor that we believe should be included in the vetting process for both ED and ER, but your vetting process must be flexible enough to handle the outcomes differently. It's great to have that choice, right? That's why, in this scenario, we love the IRS! The remainder of this chapter will focus on best practices in vetting regardless of whether you're using ED or ER.

ED or ER? A Few Sample Scenarios

Equivalency Determination	Expenditure Responsibility
Funding the purchase of assets with a long useful life (land, buildings, large equipment)	Organization is not a charitable, nonprofit entity or would not pass an ED
Development of or placement of funds into an endowment	Organization undertakes lobbying and/or political activities (though you must be 100% certain that your funds will not go toward these purposes!)
Funding an unrestricted grant purpose	If an ED was attempted and the organization did not pass, this may be your only option
Funding the development of intellectual property (for charitable purposes)	Smaller grants or short-term relationship (though this does not preclude you from undertaking ED)

Getting Started: What Documents Should You Collect from Your Grantees?

The collection of documents and an application is not (and should not be) everything in your vetting process, but it's an important starting point. The documents you collect can vary based on country, risk level, and other circumstances (again, stay away from the checklist approach!). As a baseline, we recommend collecting the following: proof of registration in-country, governing documents, audited (or unaudited) financial statements, list of the names of current board members and senior staff, and an application with a grant agreement. The agreement and application may vary depending on the program and whether you're using ED or ER. These days, nearly anyone can forge documents. So how can you trust the documents you're given? And what are some of the red flags you should look for in reviewing these documents?

Proof of Registration

We maintain an expansive *database of databases* that helps us tremendously in reviewing an organization's registration. Many countries now provide charity or tax-status search engines where you can independently verify an organization's registration. They can be difficult to find and are usually in the country's official language, but they're an invaluable asset if you can find them. You just need to set aside some time for creative online searching (or you could ask your grantee partner).

Some databases provide extensive information about organizations and their legal and financial status (good examples are the Canadian Revenue Agency Charities Listing or the UK Charity Commission site), while others will only confirm that the document you are reviewing is currently valid. Regardless, knowing that you are working with a real, registered organization is certainly a comfort and a tick-mark in the *low-risk factor* column of your review. If a database exists and you cannot find the organization listed, you should ask why. There are a variety of reasons a valid organization may not appear: you might be using the wrong database based on their registration type or region (some countries have a different site for each region or county); you may need to type the name in native language characters; *or* the explanation can be as simple as the organization you are looking for may be new, and the government does not update the site frequently. So it's always good to ask and verify before you jump to conclusions. However, if you cannot independently verify their registration, this becomes a higher risk factor and must be considered in the remainder of the review.

In vetting a registration document, it's important to review several factors:

◆ Expiration date: some countries require registration renewal or application for a new registration document every few years;

◆ Name of the law that governs: knowing what law the organization falls under may help later if the governing documents are sparse. You might find what you need in the law;

◆ Address: is the mailing address on the document the same as what the organization has given you? It may be a red flag if not; and

◆ Year of registration: an older, more established organization can be a lower risk factor. However, more recent dates may just be the registration renewal date, so it may be good to follow up on this question.

Financial Statements—Audited or Unaudited

Audited statements are certainly preferable, as they provide the reassurance that an independent party has reviewed the books to ensure accuracy and that proper accounting standards have been met. However, newer or smaller organizations may not have audited financial statements, and many countries do not require audited financials until the organization reaches a particular revenue threshold. So as not to discriminate against those organizations that may not be required to undertake or cannot afford an expensive audit, you might decide not to require audited statements. But we certainly recommend treating organizations that do not have audited statements as higher risk, and this should factor heavily in your review. It is outside of the scope of this chapter to teach the (very dull...) art of reading financials, but here are a few key questions that should be asked in this process:

◆ If they're audited, was it a clean audit?

◆ Are you looking at the most recent financial statements?

◆ Do they have a variety of different income sources? Are there any concerns with sources of income?

◆ Do they have an operating surplus? Deficit?

◆ Are there any major shifts in their numbers year over year?

◆ Is there anything questionable in their expenditures?

◆ Do their expenditures seem to be in line with the activities they were organized to undertake?

◆ Do they have a healthy asset base and reserves?

◆ How does the amount of the grant you want to send them compare to their typical income levels?

This list of questions can very easily descend into an unwieldy web of questions depending on what you uncover in the numbers. Don't be afraid to ask questions of the grantee if anything is concerning, as there may be perfectly reasonable explanations for what you're seeing. Or if you ask the right questions you might uncover a red flag that you need to know about. Foreign financial statements can sometimes look and read differently, so you need to exercise patience in this undeniably meticulous part of the vetting process. Long-term deficits, inflated sala-ries, unexplainable expenditures, and a lack of reserves could all be red flags that need to be considered in deciding whether the grantee is a good partner and could be trusted to effectively spend your grant funds. Understanding the financial health of an organization often factors heavily into the risk-based approach of the review. There are a variety of ways to manage risks that arise in the analysis of an organization's financial position. For example, if they're a small organization, you may decide a larger grant would be too risky and that it would reduce that risk if you were to pay that grant over time in smaller installments and collect reports along the way.

Governing Documents

There are several types of governing documents in different country and legal contexts (bylaws, articles of incorporation, memorandum of asso-ciation, constitution, articles of association, letters patent, charter, trust deed, etc.), and you may need to collect more than one from an organi-zation in order to find all of the information you're looking for. Reading governing documents for ED versus for ER is a very different conversa-tion, and the distinctions are mostly described within **Chapters Five** and **Six**. Even where you are undertaking ER, and the strict requirements of ED are not present, you should expect certain standards of a grantee's governance structure, or you may consider it to be a higher-risk partner. This is particularly the case if they are a charitable, nonprofit entity (and not a for-profit entity). Here are some of the most important questions you should be asking of an organization's governance structure to iden-tify any potential risk areas:

◆ Does the governing document list the purposes of the organiza-tion? If so, do they match what you have seen thus far about the organization?

◆ Does the legal name of the organization stated in the document match their registration?

◆ What will happen to the remaining funds if the organization dissolves?

◆ Does the governing document establish that the organization is a nonprofit entity and that the board of directors should receive no remuneration, dividends, or bonuses for their services?

◆ Board of Directors:

❖ How is the board structured? How many board members/ trustees are required? Do they currently have the mandatory number of members? If not, why not?

❖ How do they select their members?

❖ Do they establish how many members should be on their board at all times?

❖ How are board meetings conducted and decisions made? What is the quorum?

❖ Are the members entitled to a vote on issues presented?

❖ Who has the power on the board? Is authority evenly distributed?

It would certainly raise some red flags if you find that one person holds all of the power. For example, a board with three members that makes decisions based on a majority vote and a chairman that holds a casting vote means that one person (the chair) has the power to make all decisions. This is the type of analysis that is useful to suss out of the documents as you read them. An organization with this structure doesn't necessarily mean that there is something illicit going on, but it allows the possibility of someone abusing that power. So it is really important that you recognize such red flags and—again—apply that risk-based approach and treat this grantee more cautiously.

Tip: If the governing documents are sparse and do not contain the answers to these questions or do not contain certain provisions that you are looking for, you may need to look to the foreign laws that pertain to your grantee. If you know that your grantee is required to abide by these laws based on their registration status, reading the law could be a really good resource. Sometimes you can find the relevant laws by searching online for phrases that are found within the organization's registration document.

Background Checks: Board of Directors and Senior Staff

You can't know an organization without knowing its people. Conducting research on the board members, your contact at the organization, and the senior staff of an organization is key to helping you determine whether there is a heightened risk of money laundering, terrorist activity, bribery, fraud, or other illicit activities at the organization. **Chapter Eight** will delve into the laws that govern anti-money laundering and counter-terrorism, so here I will just focus on what you should look for in these background checks and how your findings should steer your risk-based review. The most efficient way of conducting these background checks is to subscribe to a service such as Thomson Reuters World Check, Lexis Nexis World Compliance, Fiserve, Dow Jones Watchlist, or others (the list goes on). These services provide access to a broad range of world crime lists, watchlists, lists of politically-exposed persons (PEP), and sanctions lists all within one search bar. They can be expensive, but the alternative is manually checking sanctions lists that are available online which is time-consuming and not nearly as far-reaching. You should be checking the names of board members, senior staff, and the organization name against these lists to ensure that no sanctions exist that legally prohibit you from working with an entity.

Some of your findings in these reviews may not necessarily legally prohibit you from working with someone, but it may expose your organization to more risk. For example, working with a PEP immediately increases risk, as there is a very real potential for bribery. It doesn't mean that this is happening or that you shouldn't grant to them, but it poses an inherent risk that you need to be aware of and protect yourself against. You will inevitably need to rule out *false-positive hits* especially with common names (we have had to research a "John Smith" before, no joke...), so you should be prepared to go back to the organization to ask for more identifying information if need be. Alternatively, you could do some creative online searching to see what trustworthy sources you can find about that person yourself!

Country-Specific Requirements

Vetting international charities is not only about completing the requirements for getting money out of the United States. You must also consider requirements for getting money into your grantee's country. An increasing number of countries are now monitoring foreign charitable funding and may require one of the following:

◆ Special registration that allows them to accept foreign funds (India)

◆ Government permission for each grant they receive (Egypt)

◆ Annual reporting to the government on the foreign funds they received (Bangladesh), etc.

Another increasingly important consideration are data privacy laws that are being enacted across the globe. For example, as international grantmakers, we must now collect a "model contract" from each of our European Union grantees that allows us to accept and use their *data*. Most of the time your grantees will be aware of these various requirements where they exist and can educate you, but you cannot assume that this is the case.

As a global grantmaking entity, we spend a lot of time and resources keeping up with the ever-changing nonprofit and foreign funding laws in the countries where we work. It can be a daunting and expensive task to keep up with it all. But it is very important! Where these considerations are concerned, it is very rare that you as the US grantmaker would be penalized. Instead, your grantee partners would be the ones that could face penalties if this is not managed correctly. Of course, that's the last thing we want to bring on our grantees! That is why we recommend that you add extra requirements to your process for countries where these laws exist so that you can be sure that your grantee has taken the proper steps to legally accept your funds before you grant them.

India's Foreign Contribution Regulation Act (FCRA)

◆ Every charity must register under FCRA to legally receive foreign funding.

◆ FCRA registration also dictates which bank account should be used for the fund transfer. So you also have to verify that you are sending funds to the correct account.

◆ FCRA-registered charities must file an FC-6 form annually. This reports to the government on foreign funding received during the past year. We also advise that you collect this form to ensure your grantee is in compliance.

◆ It is possible to assist a charity to obtain *prior permission* if they do not have FCRA status. This is an approval to receive funding for a specific project.

◆ In case of India, there is an online registry to verify that your grantees have their FCRA registration. We advise you to start your search there.[97]

---

[97] You can verify FCRA registration here: *fcraonline.nic.in/fc8_statewise.aspx.*

It is also important to factor the risk level of the country itself into your review. If the organization is located in a high-risk country, that automatically becomes a higher-risk factor in our review. There are a few resources that are useful to establish country risk, outside of OFAC sanctions lists. Transparency International is a good resource for this, and some of the watchlist services mentioned above have their own country risk indexes that can be a good reference. On a monthly basis, our CAF Money Laundering Risk department in London analyzes the risk level for giving to every country in the world, and to do so, they have developed a proprietary index that compiles information from a variety of different sources. We refer to this index in every review that we undertake.

How to Go Beyond the Checklist: What Other Tools Might You Have at Your Disposal?

Aside from reviewing the documents and information that your grantee actually submits to you, there are a variety of other tools you could use as a standard or on an as-needed basis to mitigate specific risks that you encounter. We recommend that you develop a list of extra vetting tools or grant controls to keep in your back pocket for enhanced due diligence or maintaining even stricter oversight over the use of your funds in higher-risk situations. Here are a few examples of extra tools we employ at CAF America and recommend that you consider in certain circumstances:

◆ Online search engines are your friend! As a standard, we always do independent online research on our grantee partners. We're looking for independent references to the work that the organization is doing through resources that are not connected to the organization or its staff themselves. If we are unable to find any independent information about our grantee, this is immediately treated as much higher risk. There may be a perfectly reasonable reason for a lack of web presence (smaller, grassroots organizations and new organizations tend not to have much presence), but it does make it more difficult to trust an organization from afar without that independent check. It's also a really good idea to search the organization's name in English and in their native language or native characters, as you will likely find more information that way. We also review Google News results for each of our grantees to ensure that there is no negative press or anything controversial going on with their work.

◆ Collection of bank statements: If an organization has unaudited (or no) financial statements, collecting bank statements may be a good alternative. This would serve as an independent resource to gain confidence in the legitimacy of the organization and to understand their current financial position.

◆ Hop on a plane! Go for a site visit! Wouldn't that be nice? You could also pay your trusted intermediary grantmaker to do it for you … (just sayin'). Really, though—many grantmakers (particularly corporate), have an international presence and likely will have a presence near their grant recipients. Employees on the ground can serve as excellent resources to either perform site visits or to vouch for the legitimacy of an organization based on local knowledge. Employees can be a great resource if this extra due diligence or reassurance is needed! It could make a riskier grantee relationship more palatable.

◆ Ask for references! If you're finished vetting an organization and are still having trouble navigating the risk factors that you've found or you are feeling like you need some extra reassurance that the organization is a good partner, it might be a good idea to do a reference check. You could ask the charity for contact information for a donor that might be willing to speak about its work, or you could approach one of its donors yourself if listed on its financials and you have a way of contacting the donor.

So What Does Your Gut Tell You? Finalizing a Review and the Approval Process

This process can really be as unscientific as just following your gut. And that can't always be expressed in a checklist. You should have a checklist to guide the review, but you should also require your charity vetting team to take detailed notes about their findings along the way and to move outside of that checklist as needed to ask questions and collect documents that are not listed there.

We also recommend that several people touch a charity review along the way, and the final reviewer should be able to fully understand the low, medium, and high-risk factors that were found throughout the review process. Was it a well-established organization with a strong web presence,

Our reviewers will typically jot some notes at the end of the review about the low and high-risk factors that were found so that they can digest what they've learned about the organization and decide what they will recommend to the final reviewers.

Case Study: The Dangers of a Checklist

A few years ago, we worked with an organization in India, founded in 1989, that provided training to smallholder farmers living under the poverty line. We followed our checklist exactly. We collected all relevant registration documents, FCRA registrations, verified their registration independently online, reviewed audited financial statements, etc. Everything completely checked out. It was a small organization that did have *some* independent web presence (though minimal). This is not entirely unusual for a small, grassroots organization. At the point where we were about to approve the review, we began receiving a number of donations for this organization, varying from $500-$2,000 (totaling about $30,000). This activity was flagged, but it still was not all that unusual for an organization which we had just vetted. The charity began calling us, asking about the status of these donations. After explaining that the due diligence process was not quite complete yet, they continued to call, though evermore persistently and aggressively. The finance team (who processed the donations), our office secretary (who was handling the calls), and the charity vetting team discussed the situation and decided that this behavior was likely a relevant factor in the review.

We began closely reviewing the donations that were coming in and noticed some strange trends in the structure of the phone numbers and email addresses, so we decided to call the donors. The phone calls all led to dead lines. We immediately reported the donations as fraud to the credit card companies and suspended the review. We determined after further review that this was, in fact, a legitimate charity, but we believe that a few bad apples at the organization had become involved in credit card fraud, and they were trying to divert the stolen funds. Catching this truly took a team of experts that were observant and sensitive to suspicious activity. We surely don't have a checkbox for that!

audited financial statements, verifiable registration, in a low-risk country? Or was it a new organization, no financial statements, small web presence, in a high-risk country? Or something in between? Which of the risk factors are you willing to accept? Are there any deal-breakers (legally or based on your organization's risk appetite)? Do you need to ask more questions and collect more information to evaluate risks or do you just need to discuss internally to decide whether you are willing to accept the risks? What would require approval from your senior staff or board? What level of risk can be approved at a staff level? When should more scrutiny be applied? It is important to develop protocols and procedures that address these questions so that you have some standards in place and some direction for how to deal with the different review outcomes that you will encounter.

Best practices in international vetting can sometimes mean standardization, but it should also mean leaving room for flexibility and creativity in your review process and decision-making. The *flexibility* aspect is qualified to of course mean *flexibility while maintaining regulatory compliance.* Vetting international charities is certainly a challenging endeavor, but if you invest time and resources into the development of a process that ensures regulatory compliance and goes further than that to build in best practices and a risk-based approach, you will be better equipped to manage the unique scenarios that will inevitably come your way. Happy vetting!

Jessie Krafft

Jessie Krafft is the Vice President of Donor Advised & Grant Services at Charities Aid Foundation of America (CAF America), where she has worked for over six years. Jessie manages the grants team responsible for charity vetting, grantmaking, and oversight of IRS regulatory compliance and foreign nonprofit laws, as well as the day-to-day support of thousands of donor clients and international charities. Under her direction, the team works diligently to remain at the forefront on all US tax laws and regulations, local foreign country regulations, and compliance-related issues in relation to international grantmaking.

Jessie holds an MA in International Development from American University. She graduated *summa cum laude* from the honors college at Virginia Commonwealth University with a BA in Spanish, a BS in Anthropology, and a minor in Latin American Studies. She holds a certificate in Nonprofit Executive Management from Georgetown University and is certified in Anti-Money Laundering (AML/CFT) by the Society of Tax and Estate Professionals (STEP). Jessie is fluent in Spanish and holds a Spanish Certificate of Translation and Interpretation from her alma mater. Before joining CAF America, she worked for eighteen months as a volunteer visitor coordinator, tutor, and child caretaker at an orphanage in Tegucigalpa, Honduras.

Chapter Eight

US Financial Transaction Laws and Their Impact on International Grantmaking

Kay Guinane and Nancy Herzog

Governments around the world have made anti-money laundering and counterterrorist financing (AML/CFT) a high priority,
both in domestic law and through the United Nations and other
multilateral bodies.[98] While the effectiveness of making AML/CFT a priority over other counterterrorism measures is a matter of debate,[99] both
governments and civil society have taken steps to prevent diversion of
charitable assets for illicit purposes.

To address the issue, there is an array of applicable laws that affect you
as grantmakers, your grantees, and the financial institutions you need to
operate programs outside the United States. These include counterterrorism laws, such as the prohibition on material support of terrorism,
laws to guard against illicit finance such as money laundering and corruption, as well as a host of economic sanctions, administered in the
United States by the Department of the Treasury (Treasury). For most
grantmakers, due diligence measures designed to comply with IRS
requirements and ensure assets are spent exclusively for charitable
purposes will be sufficient to avoid problems with these other legal/reg-
ulatory regimes. However, in some cases, the location or nature of your
programming may increase the odds that you (or your grantees) will

---

[98] Consilium, "G20 Action Plan on Countering Terrorism," accessed July 7, 2017,
consilium.europa.eu.
[99] Peter Neumann, "Don't Follow the Money: The Problem with the War on Terrorist
Financing," *Foreign Affairs*, July/August 2017, at *foreignaffairs.com.*

need to be aware of special requirements aimed at protecting national security and the financial system. This chapter reviews these special laws and the context in which they are enforced.

Risk-Based Approach

While it is important for you to understand the basic framework of AML/CFT laws that impact your operations, on a practical level it is also important to understand the context in which these laws are administered and enforced, as well as how banks cope with them. There has been a fundamental shift in the international framework since the early post-9/11 period.

In 2012 the Financial Action Task Force (FATF), a multilateral body that sets standards for laws to protect against illicit finance that are used by nearly every country, established a "risk-based approach" as the basis for AML/CFT laws and enforcement standards. This includes Recommendation 8 on nonprofits. Treasury has endorsed the risk-based approach in a variety of guidance documents, speeches and other public statements.[100] This applies to financial institutions as well as nonprofits. Treasury noted:

In addition to complying with counterterrorist financing and sanctions laws, banks should apply the risk-based approach in order to identify and manage the risks associated with a charity's transactions or accounts, just as they would for any customer. Treasury has conveyed the importance of the risk-based approach to effective implementation of controls to combat money laundering and terrorist financing.[101]

Most of the legal restrictions affecting international financial transfers were passed prior to 2012, as part of the PATRIOT Act in the years immediately following the 9/11 attacks. Most strictly prohibit *knowing* transactions with people or entities on various terrorist or sanctions lists. In other words, *there is no requirement that a grantmaker intend to support terrorism or other illegal acts for a violation to occur.* It is generally enough that the transaction sender *knows* that the recipient is on a list. (The various lists are explained below and in **Chapters Seven** and **Nine**.)

[100] Adam Szubin, "Remarks by Acting Under Secretary Adam Szubin at the ABA/ABA Money Laundering Enforcement Conference," Nov. 16, 2015, *treasury.gov.*
[101] Jennifer Fowler and Andrew N. Keller, "Joint letter from Departments of Treasury and State to the Charity & Security Network," May 13, 2016, *charityandsecurity.org.*

In its 2016 evaluation of the United States, FATF noted the inherent tension between this *strict liability standard* in the letter of the law and the flexibility that is required by the risk-based approach.[102] While the US has taken a risk-based approach to enforcement, this tension between what is possible under the strict letter of the law compared to enforcement policy remains a conundrum for grantmakers to navigate as best they can. FATF's evaluation encouraged the United States to "continue to work with the NPO community to understand and mitigate the real TF risks that exist, while engaging stakeholders on banking challenges that some NPOs may face when working in conflict zones. The US authorities are aware of the continuing challenges in this difficult area and are encouraged to continue their efforts, including work with the private sector."[103]

FATF also revised its standard on nonprofits (Recommendation 8) in June 2016 to remove language that indicated nonprofits to be *particularly vulnerable* to terrorist financing abuse and replaced it with language that requires a risk-based approach and supports the work of legitimate nonprofits. This shift was the result of advocacy by nonprofits globally, who pointed to the lack of evidence of particular vulnerability. That change, however, remains to be incorporated into legal and regulatory regimes around the globe, including Treasury's guidance for bank regulators. This transition will take time, but the overall direction favors the risk-based approach, which should work to the advantage of legitimate organizations. Treasury has noted, in its 2015 US National Terrorist Financing Risk Assessment that "there has been a shift in recent years toward individuals with no connections to a charitable organization recognized by the US government soliciting funds under the auspices of charity for a variety of terrorist groups…"[104]

During the Obama administration, enforcement authorities at Treasury and the Department of Justice told nonprofits that there was no need to change the strict liability standards in the law because prosecution of

---

[102] Financial Action Task Force, *Mutual Evaluation of the United States*, December 1, 2016, *fatf-gafi.org*.
[103] Ibid.
[104] United States Department of the Treasury, *National Terrorist Financing Risk Assessment*, July 2016 p. 43, *treasury.gov*.

legitimate nonprofits was "not an enforcement priority."[105] This had all the advantages and disadvantages of *Don't Ask Don't Tell* policies, creating a chilling effect on many nonprofits' operations while also appearing to permit latitude in legal gray areas. In fact, rather than shutting down charities using PATRIOT Act powers described below, the Obama administration primarily used civil fines and prosecution of individuals involved with nonprofits as enforcement tools.[106]

The banking sector has had a different experience with AML/CFT enforcement, which has significantly impacted its treatment of non-profit accounts. Aggressive enforcement has led to significant fines for AML/CFT violations, with the number of overall enforcement actions increasing, according to the Center for Global Development.[107] This, coupled with lack of clarity in regulatory standards and expectations, has caused many banks to avoid perceived risk by dropping accounts or subjecting transfers to extensive, delaying documentation requests. This practice, known as *derisking*, has had a significant impact on nonprofits doing international work, including grantmakers and their grantees. A February 2017 study from the Charity & Security Network found that two-thirds of US charities doing international work experience some form of problem with their banking services, affecting all types of programs working in all parts of the world.[108]

While long-term solutions are being pursued through a multistake-holder process sponsored by the World Bank and Association of Certified Anti-Money Laundering Specialists (ACAMS), in the short-term you and your grantees are likely to continue to experience problems with international transfers and related accounts. A good understanding of AML/CFT legal framework that is reflected in your due diligence procedures and understood by your bankers may help offset the effects of *derisking* while long-term solutions are put in place.

---

[105] United States Department of Justice, *Online Activities to Counter Violent Extremism*, *charityandsecurity.org*; Office of Foreign Assets Control, Department of Treasury, *Frequently Asked Questions Regarding Private Relief Efforts in Somalia* Aug. 4, 2011 Question 4, *charityandsecurity.org*.

[106] United States Department of the Treasury, "Only US charity shut down during Obama administration," February 2009, *treasury.gov*.

[107] Clay Lowry and Vijaya Ramachandran, *Unintended Consequences of Anti-Money Laundering Policies for Poor Countries*, Center for Global Development, November 2015,
p. 11 Figure 3, *cgdev.org*.

[108] Sue Eckert, Kay Guinane and Andrea Hall, *Financial Access or U.S. Nonprofits*, Charity & Security Network, February 2017, *charityandsecurity.org*.

US Financial Transaction Laws

The PATRIOT Act, passed quickly by Congress in the aftermath of the 9/11 attacks, was primarily a series of amendments to existing laws, including criminal antiterrorism laws, economic sanctions statutes and banking regulations. These changes dramatically broadened the scope of what is prohibited and expanded enforcement powers. Other relevant laws address corruption and human rights abuses.

The Prohibition on Material Support

The Antiterrorism and Effective Death Penalty Act (AEDPA) includes a broad prohibition on providing "material support" to Foreign Terrorist Organizations (FTOs) listed by the Secretary of State. The statute defines material support broadly, including:

"Any property, tangible or intangible, or service, including currency or monetary instruments or financial securities, financial services, lodging, training, expert advice or assistance, safe houses, false documentation or identification, communications equipment, facilities, weapons, lethal substances, explosives, personnel (one or more individuals who may be or include oneself), and transportation, except medicine or religious materials."[109]

Otherwise-legal financial transactions for the purposes of providing such support are included in the prohibition. The statute does *not* require that the support be *intended* to support terrorism, only that the provider *know* that the recipient is an FTO. In 2010 the Supreme Court upheld application of the prohibition to training and other assistance aimed at resolving or mitigating the effects of violent conflict.[110]

The Immigration and Nationality Act (INA) also prohibits material support[111] but applies beyond support for FTOs, covering support (1) for the commission of a terrorist activity; (2) to individuals who have committed or plan to commit terrorist activity, and (3) to terrorist organizations as defined in subsequent sections of the INA. The third category creates particular problems for nonprofits, as it is highly discretionary and the information on what groups or persons are covered is not publicly available.

---

[109] 18 USC 2339A(b).
[110] *Holder v. Humanitarian Law Project* 561 U.S. 1 (2010), 130 S.Ct. 2705.
[111] Section 212(a)(3)(B)(iv)(VI) of the Immigration and Nationality Act.

The concept of *material support* has been incorporated into sanctions in many executive orders, expanding the prohibition from the criminal to civil law.[112]

There is no humanitarian exemption. Instead, the statute has a narrow exception for medicine and religious materials.[113] Basic necessities such as food and shelter are tangible property within the meaning of the AEDPA definition. This prohibits use of an FTO as part of the aid delivery chain, even if the ultimate beneficiaries are civilians. The terms "training," "expert advice and assistance," and "personnel" suggest that "material support" could include anything from medical treatment to conflict mediation projects. In 2004 Congress passed the Intelligence Reform and Terrorism Prevention Act (IRTPA)[114] to provide greater clarity to the following three terms:

◆ Training: "instruction or teaching designed to impart a specific skill, as opposed to general knowledge."[115]

◆ Expert advice or assistance: "advice or assistance derived from scientific, technical, or other specialized knowledge."[116]

◆ Personnel: when a "person has knowingly provided, attempted to provide, or conspired to provide a foreign terrorist organization with one or more individuals (who may be or include himself) to work under that terrorist organization's direction or control or to organize, manage, supervise or otherwise direct the operation of that organization. Individuals who act entirely independently of the foreign terrorist organization to advance its goals or objectives shall not be considered to be working under the foreign terrorist organization's direction or control."[117]

AEDPA gives the secretary of state the power to exempt such nontangible forms of assistance when,[118] with the concurrence of the attorney

---

[112] See EO 13224.
[113] 18 USC 2339A(b).
[114] Intelligence Reform and Terrorism Prevention Act of 2004, Pub. L. 108-458, 118 Stat. 3638, *frwebgate.access.gpo.gov/cgi-bin/getdoc.cgi?dbname=108_cong_public_laws&docid=f:publ458.108.pdf.*
[115] 18 U.S.C. §2339A(b)(2).
[116] 18 U.S.C. §2339A(b)(3).
[117] 18 U.S.C. §2339B(h).
[118] 18 U.S.C. 2339B(j).

general, he or she determines that the assistance cannot be used to carry out terrorist activity. It is a little-used process.

In 2010 the Supreme Court reversed long-standing lower court rulings by holding that Congress can constitutionally prohibit pure speech that constitutes service, training or expert advice and assistance by peace-building organizations seeking to get terrorist groups to adopt nonviolent means of achieving their goals. The case, *Holder v. Humanitarian Law Project*[119] resulted in a bar on peacebuilding training, expert advice or assistance for listed groups.

Sanctions and Executive Orders

Over time Congress has increasingly used economic sanctions as a tool against everything from illicit finance to human rights violations. The primary authority is the International Emergency Economic Powers Act (IEEPA), passed by Congress in 1977[120] as an amendment to the Trading With the Enemy Act (TWEA). IEEPA authorizes the president to declare an emergency relating to "any unusual and extraordinary threat, which has its source in whole or in part outside the United States, to the national security, foreign policy or economy of the United States." Declarations of such threats generally take the form of an executive order against a country, individual, corporation, or other entity. Treasury administers and enforces the resulting sanctions.

To invoke the IEEPA, Section 1702(a) authorizes the president to "investigate, regulate, or prohibit" a host of financial transactions with "any foreign country or national thereof" by means of regulations, licenses, instructions, or other means. Section 1702(b) permits "investigation, block during the pendency of an investigation, regulate, direct and compel, nullify, void, prevent or prohibit" any transactions relating to property held by the designated foreign country or national."

IEEPA is the legal authority for Executive Order (EO) 13224, issued by President George W. Bush on Sept. 24, 2001. EO 13224 declared a national emergency based on the 9/11 attacks and directed Treasury, in consultation with the Attorney General and Secretary of State, to designate "Specially Designated Global Terrorists" (SDGTs) and take action to freeze all their assets subject to US jurisdiction.

---

[119] 561 U.S. 1 (2010), 130 S.Ct. 2705.
[120] 50 U.S.C. 1701-06.

Under EO 13224, designation may be of a terrorist organization, or another person or entity if Treasury finds a group:

◆ Have themselves "committed, or pose a significant threat of committing, acts of terrorism"; or

◆ Who "assist in, sponsor, or provide financial, material, or technological support," either for acts of terrorism or for persons who have committed (or pose a significant threat of committing) acts of terrorism; or

◆ Who provide "financial or other services to or in support," either of acts of terrorism or of persons who have committed (or pose a significant threat of committing) acts of terrorism; or

◆ Who are owned or controlled by any of the above persons; or

◆ Who are "otherwise associated with" persons who have committed (or pose a significant threat of committing) acts of terrorism.[121] Treasury regulations define "otherwise associated with" as (a) to own or control; or (b) to attempt, or to conspire with one or more persons, to act for or on behalf of or to provide financial, material, or technological support, or financial or other services.[122]

Between December 2001 and February 2009, nine US nonprofits were shut down under this authority. The limited appeal rights afforded to these organizations have raised serious due process issues, and the last two court cases to address the issue found that Treasury's process violates the Fifth Amendment's guarantee of due process and the Fourth Amendment's protection against warrantless searches and seizures.[123] However, the regulation on the reconsideration process has not been changed.[124]

The issue of humanitarian exemption also arises in the context of IEEPA, which bars the president from blocking "donations of food, clothing,

---

[121] George Walker Bush, "Executive Order 13224- Blocking Property and Prohibiting Transactions with Persons Who Commit, Threaten to Commit, or Support Terrorism," *Federal Register* 66, No. 186, September 25, 2001.

[122] "Terrorism Lists Governments Sanctions Regulations," 31 C.F.R. 594.316.

[123] *Al Haramain Islamic Foundation, Inc. v. United States Department of the Treasury*, 686 F.3d 965 (9th Cir. 2012); *KindHearts for Charitable and Humanitarian Development, Inc. v. Timothy Geithner*, 710 F. Supp. 2d 637 (N.D. Ohio 2010).

[124] Cherie Evans and Kay Guinane, "Mind the Gap: When It Comes To Nonprofits the Tax Code and Sanctions Regime Are In Conflict," *Tax Notes*, October 10, 2016.

and medicine, intended to be used to relieve human suffering," unless he or she determines that such donations would "seriously impair his ability to deal with any national emergency."[125] This cancellation of the humanitarian exemption was used in EO 13224 and has since become routine language in terrorism-related executive orders.[126]

In addition to terrorist designations, Treasury also administers sanctions against money launderers, drug kingpins, and others. The names of persons and entities subject to these sanctions are centralized in one list—Specially Designated Nationals (SDNs)—which is available on the Treasury website.[127] Once a person or entity is designated as an SDN, IEEPA prohibits anyone subject to US jurisdiction from carrying out any transaction with them without a license from the Office of Foreign Assets Control.

Treasury regulations permit otherwise-prohibited transactions with SDNs only through the issuance of two types of licenses:

◆ *General License* authorizing any member of the public to engage in categories of otherwise-prohibited transactions under specified terms and conditions.[128]

◆ *Specific License* authorizing, a particular actor to engage in transactions otherwise prohibited and not authorized by a general license.[129]

Treasury's website lists General Licenses on counterterrorism, provided largely for certain transactions with the Palestinian Authority. Additional General Licenses are available for some country-based sanctions, such as in Syria. Congress has also passed specific sanctions legislation that targets specific countries (such as the Iran sanctions program) as well as the Global Magnitsky Act, which targets human rights violators. The prohibition on transactions applies to these programs as well as those under IEEPA.

---

[125] 50 U.S.C. §1702(b)(2).
[126] 50 U.S.C. §1702(b)(2).
[127] "Resource Center," SDN List, US Department of Treasury, *treasury.gov/resource-center/sanctions/SDN-List/Pages/default.aspx.*
[128] 31 C.F.R. 501.801(a).
[129] 31 C.F.R. 501.801(b).

Bank Secrecy Act and FCPA

In addition to legislation that imposes limits on funding, there is legislation that requires financial institutions to assist governmental efforts to detect and prevent money laundering. The Bank Secrecy Act of 1970 (P.L. 91-508) explicitly requires that financial institutions maintain records and report designated transactions to Treasury. The Act authorizes the Secretary of the Treasury to set the reporting requirements and provides for the imposition of civil and criminal penalties for violations of the regulations. These regulations were further strengthened in the PATRIOT Act, as described above.

The Foreign Corrupt Practices Act of 1977 (FCPA) is an additional tool the US government uses to regulate international funds transfers. The FCPA makes it illegal for US entities to influence foreign officials with personal payments. In practice, the FCPA seeks to prevent US businesses from using bribery and corruption as mechanisms to further any international business interests. The FCPA was further strengthened with the International Anti-Bribery Act of 1998 which implemented provisions of the OECD Anti-Bribery Convention.

Enforcement and Administration

Noncompliance with sanctions and transactions with restricted entities may result in civil or criminal penalties. Enforcement of US government sanctions programs is the responsibility of the Office of Foreign Assets Control (OFAC) at the Treasury Department. IEEPA allows the president to choose among a variety of sanctions, including criminal or civil penalties. Civil penalties can include investigations, regulations, and control over transactions.[130] The Department of Justice oversees criminal prosecutions for violations of the material support prohibition. Penalties for violations are severe: up to 20 years in prison or more, if death results, and fines of up to $500,000 for organizations and $250,000 for individuals.[131]

Grantmakers whose operations may involve locations or contact with sanctioned persons or entities should consult the Treasury SDN list to avoid engaging in prohibited transactions that could lead to enforcement action against them and to determine when it is appropriate to act

---

[130] "Presidential Authorities," 50 U.S.C. §1702(a)(1)(B).
[131] "Providing Material Support or Resources to Designated Foreign Terrorist Organizations" 18 U.S.C. § 2339B.

under a general license for grantmaking activity or if a special license might be needed.

Practitioner Tips

In the wake of increased regulations and attention to international transactions, you can implement practices to minimize potential disruption to your efforts to fund programs. Education and awareness are the cornerstone of best practices and the most effective means of safeguarding both programs and funds.

There are some practical steps you as a grantmaker may take to ensure overall compliance with regulations:

Educate Staff and Board on the Compliance Requirements and Risks Posed by Noncompliance

If those responsible for oversight and administration of grantmaking are not familiar with the compliance requirements, it will be impossible to achieve satisfactory compliance. Make sure that the board and senior leadership are aware of the requirements, and that new staff—in program, grants management, and finance positions—are informed as well, at least in a general sense. Staff with specific responsibilities related to compliance must be aware of the specifics and can serve as a resource for the organization.

Compliance is most easily done when it is part of routine operations. For example, conducting a watchlist search on grant applicants can be incorporated as a step in the grant approval process. Similarly, a watchlist search on payees can be made part of an organization's internal controls prior to making payments.

If a grantmaker's programs include funding projects in or related to any sanctioned countries or areas where designated non-state groups operate, additional actions are needed. Education and awareness are key in this area as well. The following should be considered:

Review the List of Sanctions

The OFAC website includes detailed listings and explanatory documents related to all US government sanctions. Review this information to determine if any programs or recipients are in areas of concern. Read this information carefully. In most cases, sanctions apply to transactions that are *directly* or *indirectly* supportive of the country or SDN in question. This means, for example, that sanctions may very well apply to a grant recipient in France whose funded project is supporting activities in the Boko Haram-controlled area of Nigeria, even if no funds are being transferred to Nigeria.

Stay Up-to-Date and Sign Up for Alerts on OFAC Updates

OFAC offers instant notifications on any new actions related to sanctions. It is easy to check for new information or sign up for email notifications on the Treasury website.

Determine If a License Is Needed Before Issuing a Grant Award

If the funded project falls under a sanctions program, review the OFAC materials carefully.

- ◆ If there is an OFAC general license and it provides sufficient coverage of the funded activities, cite this license in the grant award for clarity. This will be useful to both you as the grantor and your grantee if there are questions from an auditor, a financial institution, or other parties.

- ◆ If there is not a general license or if it does not cover the activities to be funded, you must decide whether to proceed with the program by applying for a Specific License, which may take some time. The procedures for applying and additional information can be found at the OFAC website.

Consider Working with Intermediaries

If a grantmaker does not have the capacity or the will to manage licensing and compliance, it may decide to work with an intermediary which can manage these processes on their behalf. An intermediary may take a variety of forms, from a pass-through recipient who will work with the recipient under a subgrant arrangement to an organization that provides complete grants management services.

When an award is made to a recipient outside of the United States, the successful transfer of funds is a vital component of a project's success. International transfers may be complicated, even if the recipient is not in a location affected by sanctions. With this, awareness and education are key as well.

Understand Banking Processes

Make sure that the staff involved with approving and processing wire transfers understand the entire process of how the funds go from the donor's bank account in the United States to the recipient's foreign bank account. International transfers involve more steps than domestic wires or Automated Clearing House (ACH) payments. This includes correspondent accounts, intermediary accounts, and currency exchange. Having an understanding of the steps along the way will help ensure that the correct information is gathered and transmitted to the financial institutions involved.

Educate International Grantees about the Wire Transfer Process

The success of an international wire transfer often depends on the quality of the information that is included in the wire transfer instructions. Incomplete or inaccurate account numbers, IBANs, correspondent account information, or translation or transliteration of account names may cause delays or even refusals of wire transfers. Recipients with little experience with US donors may not know how to present their account information to facilitate successful transfers. It is worth the time and effort to assist them with bank literacy, to ensure the quality of the information provided as well as to facilitate their communication and problem solving with their local bank.

Cite a License in Payment Instructions, Where Applicable

If the project is authorized under a General or Specific license from OFAC, include this information with the bank account data sent along with the wire transfer request. This may help save time from delay caused by the bank's compliance department if the transfer is flagged for compliance review.

Make Friends with Your Bank

Having a good working relationship with representatives of your banking institution will facilitate a quicker exchange of information as well as possible minimization of compliance reviews of wire transfer requests. If a banking partner is familiar with the type of work and institutions normally funded by the grantmaker, the bank may be able to make quicker judgment calls on compliance questions and may be more effective at solving problems with intermediary financial institutions along the way.

Work with More Than One Financial Institution

Each bank has its own compliance department with its own assessment of risks and internal rules and guidelines. You may find that one bank will not accept wire transfers to a sanctioned country, even with a

Specific License, whereas another one will. If your grantmaking program involves multiple countries, you may find that one financial institution may not meet all of the needs of your program.

Consider Wire Transfers in Non-USD Currency

As a wire transfer works its way through the process, the various correspondent banks along the way each perform a compliance review and risk assessment. These processes may vary dependent on the currency of the transaction, especially during the final transfer to the recipient's account. A transfer in Euros or local currency may have an easier time than a transfer in US dollars, as the assessed risk of money laundering may be lower.

Set Realistic Expectations for Timing of Funds Transfers

Be clear with recipients that international transfers may take several days in the best of circumstances, and several weeks if there are compliance holds in any part of the process. Make sure they and you plan for this as part of the grant payment schedule.

Investigate Alternate Payment Methods

The standard wire transfer to the recipient organization's bank account is not the only way to send funds to international grantees. When circumstances make the standard difficult or even impossible, look into other ways to send funds. Options may include transfers to individual bank accounts, utilization of cash transfer services such as Western Union, wire transfers through intermediary organizations, or individuals who can pass the funds to the recipient, cryptocurrencies, or even cash payments.[132] Each option may come with its own set of risks, which can be mitigated through strong internal controls and award terms.

And, last but certainly not least:

Network with Other Grantmakers to Share Knowledge and Experiences

If your organization is having difficulty with international wire transfers, you can be certain that others are as well. Other grantmakers are often the best source of information for advice, tips, and best practices to work through the difficulties. Make use of the professional grants management networks to share experiences. As privacy is often a con-

---

[132] Note legal requirement regarding carrying more than $10,000 in cash or financial instruments.

cern, be aware that it is possible to share information about mechanisms and experiences with various financial institutions without divulging any information about specific projects, grantees, or bank account information.

AML/CFT Resources

USA PATRIOT Act	*https://www.gpo.gov/fdsys/ pkg/PLAW-107publ56/pdf/ PLAW-107publ56.pdf*	Text of the law
OFAC Sanctions	*https://www.treasury.gov/ resource-center/sanctions/ Pages/default.aspx*	List and full text of sanctions and guidance resources
OFAC Licenses	*https://www.treasury.gov/ resource-center/sanctions/ Pages/licensing.aspx*	Information and tool for applying for a specific license
SDN List	*https://www.treasury.gov/ resource-center/sanctions/ SDN-List/Pages/default.aspx*	Searchable SDN lists and guidance
FinCen	*https://www.fincen.gov*	Information about the mission and activities of the US agency charged with enforcement of AMT/CFL regulations

Kay Guinane, JD

Kay Guinane is a public interest attorney who specializes in the rights of nonprofit organizations, particularly in the areas of free speech, association, and national security. As Director of the Charity & Security Network, she leads efforts to make national security rules impacting nonprofit organizations consistent with constitutional and human rights principles and to eliminate unnecessary barriers to their legitimate work.

She has published research, testified before Congress and the Federal Election Commission, and engaged extensively in advocacy and consulting on these issues in the United States and abroad. She serves as Co-Chair of the Global NPO Coalition on FATF.

Kay holds BA and JD degrees from the State University of New York at Buffalo and is licensed to practice law in the District of Columbia, Kentucky, and Maryland.

Nancy Herzog

Nancy Herzog is the Senior Director of Grants Administration at the National Endowment for Democracy, where she leads a team responsible for ensuring compliance and effective and efficient grants management of NED's global grantmaking program, which makes about 1,500 grants annually in more than eighty countries.

She has served on the board of PEAK Grantmaking and is an active participant and presenter at conferences and related events in the grants management field. Nancy received a BA from Wesleyan University in Russian Studies and an MA in International Policy Studies from the Middlebury Institute of International Studies at Monterey.

Chapter Nine

Responsible Giving: The International Grantmakers' Perspective

Jane Peebles

The penalties for violating US anti-terrorist financing rules are severe. The government can freeze your nonprofit's assets and revoke its tax-exempt status even if you never intended to support terrorism and have no idea charitable dollars have been diverted for this purpose. Some of the rules are vague and broad, so it's hard to figure out how to comply. The government hasn't offered the nonprofit sector any *safe-harbor* set of procedures that will definitely insulate you from liability if you inadvertently allow funds or supplies to be diverted for terrorist purposes.

Nonprofits that are funding charitable projects abroad are generally at higher risk of having goods or funds diverted than domestic grantmakers are. It's simply harder to monitor what happens abroad than to track how a US nonprofit uses your grant. If you are funding a large, well-known charity abroad, the grantee will most likely already have a culture of accountability that includes financial transparency and regular reporting back to the grantmaker. But if you are funding new or small charities abroad, particularly in politically unstable, corrupt, or war-torn areas, tracking your dollars can be extremely difficult.

This chapter will offer insight into and reasons for many uncertainties about how to comply with the anti-terrorist financing rules, what voluntary best practices and other guidance our government has offered, and why nonprofits and their advisors with first-hand experience in cross-border grantmaking have objected to certain government guidelines. I will describe and explain pragmatic best-practice compliance procedures that leaders in the US nonprofit sector are implementing. I'll walk you through funding projects abroad in a manner that best minimizes the risk of diversion of funds or supplies by terrorists and terrorist organizations. I'll wrap up with practical, real-life examples of what to do and not to do.

> Violating anti-terrorist financing rules can result in fifteen years in prison, life in prison, retroactive loss of tax-exempt status, civil liability and freezing of your nonprofit's assets. You don't want to learn the hard way!

Most of us think about laws against financing terrorism and assisting terrorists, if at all, in the context of the September 11, 2001, terrorist attacks on US soil. We had laws against financing terrorism before 9/11, but the post-9/11 press coverage about terrorists followed by the government suddenly freezing the assets of several Muslim charities operating in the US garnered a lot of attention. Continuing random terrorist attacks at home and abroad have kept this issue very much in the public eye.

Shortly after 9/11, then-President George W. Bush signed Executive Order 13224.[133] EO 13224 directs the Department of the Treasury's Office of Foreign Asset Control (OFAC) to maintain a list of known and suspected terrorists and terrorist organizations, who are referred to in the order as "Listed Persons." As **Chapter Eight** discussed in detail, EO 13224 allows blocking of assets of suspected terrorists listed in the executive order, people determined by the Secretary of State to have committed or be likely to commit terrorist actions, people who are "controlled by" or "act for or on behalf of" suspected or confirmed terrorists and terrorist organizations, and people who support them or are "otherwise associated with" them. EO 13224 prohibits anyone in the United States from providing funds, goods, or services to Listed Persons, including humanitarian donations of food, potable water, and the like. Section three of EO 13224 defines *terrorism* as an activity that (i) involves a violent act or an act dangerous to human life, property, or infrastructure; and (ii) appears

---

[133] Executive Order 13224, "Blocking Property and Prohibiting Transactions With Persons Who Commit, Threaten to Commit or Support Terrorism," 31 C.F.R. §594 (Sept. 25, 2001). While not technically a law, Executive Order 13224 has the force of law.

to be intended (A) to intimidate or coerce a civilian population; (B) to influence the policy of a government by intimidation or coercion; or (C) to affect the conduct of government by mass destruction, assassination, kidnapping, or hostage-taking.

Executive Order 13224 also authorizes OFAC to freeze the assets of any US person or entity that intentionally or *unwittingly* engages in transactions involving (i) Listed Persons, (ii) their property, or (iii) unnamed persons who assist, sponsor, or provide financial support or humanitarian aid to, or are otherwise associated with, Listed Persons, or who are suspected of doing so.

Concerns about Complying with Anti-Terrorist Financing Rules

While not technically a law, EO 13224 has the force of law and it applies to US nonprofits. A nonprofit's assets can be frozen, and its tax-exempt status revoked, even if it is just suspected of *inadvertently* having supported terrorism.[134] The asset freeze will continue pending the outcome of an investigation into whether the nonprofit supports terrorism. OFAC purposely doesn't give any advance warning before freezing a nonprofit's assets. If a terrorist organization had advance warning, it might conceal its assets or transfer them out of the country, beyond our government's jurisdiction.

The earliest lists of terrorists and terrorist organizations were a part of Executive Order 13224. Now, the primary US terrorist list is the so-called Specially Designated Nationals List (the SDN List) maintained by OFAC. The SDN List is very long and changes constantly. Any nonprofit on the SDN List immediately and retroactively loses its tax-exempt status and can no longer solicit or accept donations from US sources. No US person or entity may engage in any transaction with a Listed Person.[135]

---

[134] If your nonprofit is just being formed, include provisions in your bylaws or governing trust instrument describing the procedures you plan to adopt to minimize the risk of diversion of funds to support terrorism. Your entity's application for tax-exempt status (currently IRS Form 1023) must indicate whether you plan to make grants to support charitable projects abroad. In an attachment to the application, reiterate what risk-based procedures your nonprofit will implement to protect against inadvertently providing goods or services to terrorists or terrorist organizations.

[135] See **Chapter Eight** for permitted exceptions: general and specific licenses.

Moreover, a month after Executive Order 13224 was signed, Congress amended and strengthened the PATRIOT Act,[136] which imposes civil and criminal penalties on nonprofits and their directors if they are found to have *intentionally* provided "material support" to terrorists. The amendment to the PATRIOT Act strengthened the Antiterrorism and Effective Death Penalty Act of 1996 to expand its list of terrorist-type offenses and impose harsher penalties on US persons who provide material support to terrorists intending that their support be used to commit a terrorist offense.[137]

Under the statutes, "material support" means providing "any property, tangible or intangible, or service." The term includes currency, financial services, lodging, training, expert advice or assistance, safe houses, false identification, communications equipment, facilities, weapons, lethal substances, explosives, personnel, transportation, and other physical assets except medicine or religious materials.[138]

It should be noted that the US had anti-terrorist financing laws long before 9/11. Laws passed in the mid-1990s gave teeth to the Justice Department's terrorist prosecution efforts. These pre-9/11[139] statutes outlaw knowingly providing material support for the commission of certain terrorist offenses and knowingly providing material support to certain designated terrorist organizations. Congress has amended both of these laws over the years.

Nonprofits, while aware of the regulations, remain unsure how to comply and concerned that there are no safe-harbor measures they can adopt to avoid being identified as supporters of terrorists or otherwise associated with terrorists.

Let us look at some of the reasons for the many uncertainties about how to comply with the rules and at how the Department of the Treasury (Treasury) has tried to help the nonprofit sector by (i) recommending voluntary best practices and (ii) providing a tool for assessing the risk

---

[136] The USA PATRIOT Act of 2001, "Uniting and Strengthening America by Providing Appropriate Tools Required to Intercept and Obstruct Terrorism;" Pub. L. No. 107-56, 115 Stat. 272 (2001).

[137] **Chapter Eight** discusses Executive Order 13224 and the PATRIOT Act in much more detail.

[138] 18 U.S.C. §2333, §2339B.

[139] 18 U.S.C. §2339A(b).

of whether a grant intended for use abroad might end up in the wrong hands.

These are just a sample of the nonprofit sector's concerns that may very well resonate with you as an international grantmaker:

◆ How can we identify "unnamed persons" who assist terrorists?

◆ How can we identify unnamed persons who are "otherwise associated with terrorists" but haven't assisted, sponsored, or provided humanitarian aid or financial support to terrorists?

◆ Can "persons who are otherwise associated with" terrorists include persons or entities to which the grantee may re-grant funds? Can it include vendors used by the grantee?

◆ Executive Order 13224 defines "terrorism" to include "an activity that—(ii) appears to be intended (A) to intimidate or coerce a civilian population." Could this apply to legitimate political protests?

Government Resources and Guidance on Compliance with Anti-Terrorist Financing Laws

After OFAC froze the assets of three important Muslim charities operating in the United States in 2001,[140] other Muslim charities asked for guidance on how to avoid having their assets frozen. In response to this request, in November 2002 Treasury issued "Anti-Terrorist Financing Guidelines: Voluntary Best Practices for US-Based Charities" (the "2002 Voluntary Guidelines"). Nonprofits with international activities and their professional advisors closely studied the 2002 Voluntary Guidelines. Their detailed analysis caused many experts in cross-border philanthropy much consternation and uncertainty. OFAC intended the 2002 Voluntary Guidelines to help cross-border grantmakers and providers of humanitarian aid comply with Executive Order 13224. However, while the 2002 Voluntary Guidelines offer lots of helpful recommendations, many in the charitable sector found several of the suggested *best practices* to be vague, overbroad, unrealistic, or impossible to implement.

---

[140] *See Holy Land Foundation for Relief and Development v. Ashcroft*, 333 F.3rd 156 (D.C. Cir. 2003), *cert denied*, 72 U.S.L.W. 3551 (2004); *Benevolence International Foundation, Inc. v. O'Neill*, 200 F.Supp. 2nd 935 (N.D. Ill. 2002); and *Global Relief Foundation, Inc. v. O'Neill*, 315 F.3rd 748 (7th Cir.), *cert denied* 124 S.Ct. 531 (2003).

The preamble to the 2002 Voluntary Guidelines, as revised in 2006, makes clear that following the guidelines is *not a safe harbor* from liability for assisting terrorists or providing material support to terrorist organizations:

> *[A]dherence to these Guidelines does not excuse any person (individual or entity) from compliance with any local, state, or federal law or regulation, nor does it release any person from or constitute a legal defense against any civil or criminal liability for violating any such law or regulation. In particular, adherence to these Guidelines shall not be construed to preclude any criminal charge, civil fine, or other action by Treasury or the Department of Justice against persons who engage in prohibited transactions with persons designated pursuant to the Antiterrorism and Effective Death Penalty Act of 1996, as amended, or with those that are designated under the criteria defining prohibited persons in the relevant executive orders issued pursuant to statute, such as the International Emergency Economic Powers Act, as amended.*

The 2002 Voluntary Guidelines recommended steps that Treasury thought all grantmakers should follow before making grants to any foreign grantee. The recommendations cover both information you should request from the grantee and due diligence your nonprofit should conduct on its own. Treasury recommended the following:

◆ Conducting a basic vetting of the foreign grantee, including checking to make sure it did not appear on any government lists identifying parties with links to terrorism or money laundering, and

◆ Reviewing the financial operations of the foreign grantee.

Many components of these steps are familiar as routine pre-grant inquiries required under the Internal Revenue Code. Appropriate due diligence includes gathering data about a proposed foreign grantee to verify questions such as: Does it have the capacity to carry out the project? Is it a charity under the laws of its home jurisdiction? Does it have appropriate governing documents? Is its charitable purpose one recognized as such under Internal Revenue Code section 501(c)(3)? The 2002 Voluntary Guidelines, however, went far beyond the usual pre-grant inquiries, due diligence, ongoing expenditure responsibility or other grantmaker oversight of the use of a grant. They imposed responsibility for avoiding terrorist financing through nonprofit channels squarely on the shoulders of nonprofit grantmakers.

Treasury formulated and published the 2002 Voluntary Guidelines *without any input* from the nonprofit sector. The guidelines engendered substantial comments and criticism from the nonprofit community. In the face of these objections, in May 2003, Treasury invited the sector to submit further comments and to formulate alternate recommendations and guidelines for minimizing the chance of diversion of nonprofits' funds or supplies to terrorism.[141] In 2003, the Council on Foundations, the American Bar Association and several others submitted comments on the 2002 Voluntary Guidelines to Treasury.

According to some of the critics,[142] the 2002 Voluntary Guidelines failed to accomplish the objective of guarding charitable funds from diversion to terrorist activities without "killing legitimate good works" because they adopted a one-size-fits-all approach which would greatly increase the administrative costs of making international grants without helping US nonprofits identify and take appropriate precautions with respect to the small number of grants for use abroad that are actually at risk for diversion. A common comment was that the 2002 Voluntary Guidelines failed to recognize that the data grantmakers should collect from the grantee might vary based on several factors, including the size of the grantee, whether the grantmaker has had a long-standing relationship with it, whether the grantee is based in a high-risk area, and what steps the grantmaker has already taken to minimize the risk that its funds may be diverted from its mission and charitable purpose.

In response, Treasury released draft revised voluntary guidelines in 2005 (the "2005 Voluntary Guidelines") for further public comment. The 2005 Voluntary Guidelines adopted some of the recommendations of the Council on Foundations and others, but they also imposed even more onerous data collection guidelines. Moreover, although they are referred to as *voluntary guidelines*, the nonprofit sector was concerned that other government agencies would come to see the suggestions in the revised 2005 Voluntary Guidelines as a minimum standard.

The 2005 Voluntary Guidelines

The 2005 Voluntary Guidelines state they are intended to assist charities in developing a risk-based approach to guard against the diversion of charitable funds for use by terrorists and their supporting networks.

---

[141] I.R.S. Ann. 2003-29, 2003-20 I.R.B. 928.
[142] See Council on Foundations, "Comments on U.S. Department of the Treasury Anti-Terrorist Financing Guidelines: Voluntary Best Practices for U.S.-Based Charities."

Section VI of the 2005 Voluntary Guidelines, offering anti-terrorist financing best practices, recommends that nonprofits collect the following "basic information" about the foreign grantee before distributing any charitable funds or in-kind contributions:

◆ The foreign organization's name in English and the language of origin, and any current or other names used to identify the recipient;

◆ The jurisdictions in which the foreign organization maintains a physical presence;

◆ Information regarding the individuals who formed the foreign organization and the organization's operating history;

◆ Data regarding each place of business of the foreign organization (not just its principal place of business);

◆ A statement of the foreign organization's principal purpose, including a detailed report of its projects and goals;

◆ The names and addresses of individuals, entities, or organizations to which the foreign organization provides or proposes to provide funding, services or material support, to the extent reasonably available;

◆ The names and addresses of any subcontracting organizations utilized by the foreign organization;

◆ Copies of all public filings or releases made by the foreign organization, including official registry documents, annual reports, and annual filings with the government, as applicable; and

◆ The foreign organization's sources of income.

Under the revised 2005 Voluntary Guidelines, basic vetting of recipients would involve:

◆ A reasonable search of public information, including information available online, to determine whether the foreign organization is suspected of terrorist activity, including terrorist financing or other support;

◆ Checking of the OFAC SDN list;

◆ Obtaining the full name in English, the language of origin, and the acronym or the names used by, nationality, citizenship, current country of residence and place and date of birth of key employees, board members, or other senior management of the foreign organization's principal place of business, and key employees of the foreign organization's other business locations;

◆ Consulting publicly available information to ensure that key employees, board members, or other senior management of the foreign organization are not suspected of activity relating to terrorism; and

◆ Imposing a requirement that the foreign organization certify that it does not employ, transact with, provide services to or otherwise deal with any individuals, entities, or groups that are sanctioned by OFAC or with any persons known to the recipient to support terrorism.

The recommendation that US grantmakers require a foreign grantee to certify that it does not support terrorism seemed absurd to some in the charitable sector. Would any foreign grantee refuse to sign such a certification? Refusal would lead the grantmaker to the inevitable conclusion that the proposed grantee was a terrorist group or filtered funds to terrorists. Ultimately, some of the largest funders, such as the Ford Foundation and MacArthur Foundation, started including this certification requirement in their policies and grant agreements. It is one of the simpler practices recommended by the 2005 Voluntary Guidelines, and (i) demonstrates an effort to comply with the guidelines and (ii) puts recognition of the risk of inadvertently supporting terrorism firmly front and center.

Additional guidelines suggest that the US nonprofit should conduct basic vetting of its own key employees and, if it finds one of its own employees or anyone connected with the foreign recipient organization on the OFAC SDN list, report the match to OFAC. If such data are gleaned from a source other than the OFAC SDN list, they are to be reported to the Department of the Treasury and to the Federal Bureau of Investigation.

Led by the Council on Foundations, a Treasury Guidelines Working Group (TGWG) was assembled to both offer comments and propose more reasonable and workable alternatives to combat terrorist financing. The TGWG was made up of over forty highly regarded nonprofits and advisors to nonprofits. The TGWG developed the "Principles of

International Charity" as a pragmatic alternative to the revised 2005 Voluntary Guidelines in part because it was extremely concerned that these continued to suggest "onerous and potentially harmful procedures to charities." The TGWG concluded that the 2005 Voluntary Guidelines suggested the collection of more information on more individuals and organizations than the 2002 Voluntary Guidelines, that it is impossible for nonprofits to collect that information, and that, even if they were able to, the costs of doing so would be prohibitive. They also expressed substantial concern that the 2005 Voluntary Guidelines do not, in fact, reflect the voluntary best practices of US nonprofits. The "Principles of International Charity" were submitted to Treasury with a request that Treasury revoke the 2005 Voluntary Guidelines and adopt the "Principles of International Charity" in their place.[143]

The 2006 Voluntary Guidelines

Treasury was not receptive to revoking the 2005 Voluntary Guidelines or adopting the "Principles of International Charity" in their place. Instead, in September of 2006, Treasury released a set of revised Anti-Terrorist Financing Guidelines addressing some of the comments received in response to the 2005 Voluntary Guidelines. In these further revised guidelines (the "2006 Voluntary Guidelines"), Treasury made it very clear that adhering to the 2006 Voluntary Guidelines is *not a safe harbor* and, conversely, failure to adhere to them does not, *in and of itself*, constitute a violation of US law. The 2006 Voluntary Guidelines reflect Treasury's recognition that a one-size-fits-all approach is "untenable and inappropriate" due to the diversity of grantmakers, their operations, and circumstances. Treasury also acknowledged that in certain circumstances, such as a first responder to catastrophic disaster relief, it is "difficult" for a grantmaker to adhere to the guidelines.

One of the concerns of the nonprofit community was that Treasury's recommendations would endanger humanitarian aid workers on the ground if they were perceived as instruments of the US government and, so, distrusted. The 2006 Voluntary Guidelines specify that "[c]harities are independent entities and are not part of the US Government." Nonetheless, the 2006 Voluntary Guidelines were still troubling to the TGWG. The Council on Foundations' comments on the 2006 Voluntary Guidelines, expressed by then-President of the Council on Foundations

---

[143] See press release entitled "US Charities Call for US Department of Treasury to Withdraw Anti-Terrorist Financing Guidelines," February 21, 2016, *www.cof.org*.

Steve Gunderson, in a letter to then-Secretary of the Treasury Henry Paulson, Jr.,[144] pointed out these continuing concerns:

◆ "The guidelines specifically exaggerate the extent to which US charities have served as a source of terrorist funding."

◆ "The guidelines continue to impose onerous information collection and reporting requirements that do little to protect charities from terrorist abuse."

◆ "Treasury has not gone far enough to ensure that the guidelines remain voluntary."

Treasury Risk Matrix for the Charitable Sector

OFAC published a Risk Matrix for the Charitable Sector (the "Matrix") on its website in March 2007. OFAC made no public announcement regarding the Matrix and did not offer a draft of the Matrix for a public comment period prior to its publication. The introduction to the Matrix says it is needed because "reports by international organizations and the media have revealed the vulnerability of the charitable sector to abuse by terrorists." It continues by highlighting that the Matrix will be "particularly useful for charities that conduct overseas charitable activities due to increased risks associated with international activities." Furthermore, the Matrix again stresses the government's opinion that "terrorists, rogue actors and other sanctions targets" take advantage of grantmakers and that the vulnerability of US grantmakers threatens our national security.

The introduction notes that the Matrix is not a comprehensive list, and it clarifies in footnote 1 that use of the Matrix is not mandatory. Instead, footnote 1 recognizes that "charities and their grantees differ from one another in size, products, and services, sources of funding, the geographic locations that they serve, and numerous other variables." However, the burden is on charities to determine the best approach, since Treasury still has no safe harbors or specific measures that protect against sanctions including asset seizure. According to footnote 3, Treasury "addresses every violation in context, taking into account the nature of a charity's business, the history of the group's enforcement

---

[144] Acting on behalf of the TGWG, Steve Gunderson wrote Henry M. Paulson, Jr. on December 18, 2006. "Nonprofits Ask Treasury to Withdraw Anti-Terrorist Financing Guidelines," Guidestar Blog, Suzanne Coffman, January 1, 2017.

record with OFAC, the sanctions harm that may have resulted from the transaction, and the charity's compliance procedures."[145]

The Matrix lists eleven factors according to which it can be established whether there is a low, medium, or high risk of diversion of funds to terrorists or terrorist organizations. The risk analysis is based on whether the following factors exist:

1. Specificity of the grantee's stated purpose and expenditures

2. A written grant agreement with safeguards against diversion of funds

3. An existing relationship between the US charity and the foreign grantee

4. Reliable references for the foreign grantee

5. Grantee history of legitimate activities

6. Adequate due diligence by the grantmaker, including on-site review and audits

7. Provision by the grantee of its governing documents, local law, and other requested documents

8. The size of fund disbursements

9. The availability and use of a reliable banking system

10. Suspension procedures developed by the grantmaker so funding is cut off if the grantmaker learns or suspects funds have been diverted, and

11. The location of charity's work (US only, international, conflict areas)

In footnote 4, Treasury notes that the Matrix should be applied to subgrantees "to the extent reasonably practicable."

As you may expect, the Matrix was also controversial. Grantmakers Without Borders[146] complained in a letter to Treasury that the Risk

---

[145] Risk Matrix for the Charitable Sector, March 2007.
[146] Grantmakers Without Borders is a philanthropic network of more than 150 organizations.

Matrix casts unfair suspicion on small grassroots nonprofits working in conflict-ridden areas.[147] Again, US international grantmakers were frustrated with Treasury's failure to confer with the nonprofit community regarding the Risk Matrix.

Voluntary Compliance Best Practices

The easiest voluntary measure to comply with is checking the proposed grantee and its directors against the OFAC SDN list. You can access a searchable SDN List on OFAC's website. It is long and changes constantly. Due to the vagaries of transliteration and the similarities or very common use of certain foreign names, *false positives* do come up. There isn't much to do if the name of a director of a foreign grantee is as common as John Smith is in the United States. If a false positive comes up, you can also check the Department of Justice's US Government Terrorist Exclusion List ("TEL") kept for TSA and immigration purposes, as well as the lists maintained by the United Nations and the European Union. The lists generally include variant spellings and aliases.

Although Treasury did not adopt the "Principles of International Charity," you may find them to be very useful. They recommend a risk-based approach to grantmaking which (i) helps the grantmaker to identify those grants that may present a greater risk for diversion and (ii) describes additional steps the grantmaker may take to minimize the possibility of diversion for higher-risk grants. They set forth reasonable guidelines which may vary according to circumstance. The "Principles

Check the lists:

◆ Specially Designated Nationals List (SDN List) maintained by the Office of Foreign Assets Control—*Always!*

◆ Terrorist Exclusion List (TEL) maintained by Department of Justice

◆ United Nations Consolidated List

◆ European Union Terrorist List

Note that lists often overlap and there is no free single consolidated list. All lists are searchable online.

Tip: Retain all results of list searches, even those returning no results.

---

[147] Kay Guinane, "U.S. Counterterrorism Developments Impacting Charities," *The International Journal of Not-for-Profit Law*, Vol. 10, Issue 1, December 2007.
[148] See more about the available lists in **Chapter Seven**.

of International Charity" recommend that, depending on the circumstances, in addition to the usual due diligence, the international grantmaker may employ a number of supplementary practices. These practices include, but are not limited to:

◆ Supplementing its pre-grant investigation by checking its grantees and their board members against the terrorist lists and/or requiring grantees to certify that they have not and will not knowingly provide material support or resources for acts of violence or terrorism

◆ Disbursing large grants in semiannual installments, with successive payments contingent upon receipt and satisfactory review of six-month interim reports (rather than the usual annual financial and progress reports required from grantees)

◆ For a small US grantmaking organization with no overseas staff which has been funding an organization abroad for many years and has developed a close working relationship with the grantee over time, the use of formal grant agreements specifying the charitable purposes for which each grant may be used, regular monitoring reports from the grantee, and periodic site visits and project assessments by the grantmaker, a consultant, or another reputable organization on the grantmaker's behalf

◆ For a US-based relief or development organization with overseas staff, reliance on its knowledge of the community and its continuing presence there to have confidence that its pre-grant investigation and subsequent monitoring of the use of the grant are sufficient to reduce the risk of diversion of charitable funds. If a grantmaker does not have an established relationship with a new grantee, it might decide that additional inquiry regarding the bona fides of the board members and key employees of the grantee, and requiring a certification that it will not finance terrorism, are appropriate

◆ For a US corporation that has an employee match giving program, the delegation of the due diligence to a knowledgeable vendor, with a requirement that the vendor supplements its usual practices to verify that the grantee organizations do not appear on any list of terrorists or terrorist organizations

Case Studies

School for Girls in Africa

Your US nonprofit wants to support a small school for girls in Africa. The school is applying for charitable status under local law. Working with local African counsel, you determine that neither local law nor the school's governing document, its memorandum of association, requires that if the school ever stops operating, all of its remaining assets must be distributed to another charity. Local counsel provides you with the following first-year budget for the school:

    $xx   Legal fees

    $x   Filing and permit fees

    $xx   First-year teacher salary

    $x   Supplies (specified items and prices)

    $1/2x   Miscellaneous

When you inquire about the miscellaneous funds, the local counsel tells you that they are for members of the village council who are to approve the school's application for charitable status and that "otherwise it will take much longer."

The founder of your nonprofit has visited the school several times, met several students and knows and trusts the teacher. She has made prior nondeductible direct gifts to the school. Your founder's first-hand knowledge of the school, its prior history, and its staff provides reassurance that grant funds for school operations will be used for legitimate educational purposes that will further your mission.

Can the hurdles be overcome?

Assuming that your nonprofit has already received all of the data it requested from the grantee, find out from local counsel whether it is permissible to amend the memorandum of association to include the necessary dissolution clause. If not, would a certification in the grant agreement that any remaining assets would be granted to another charity be binding on the grantee?

If the miscellaneous *facilitation fees* are intended to motivate a local council member to bring the application for tax-exempt status of the grantee in its home jurisdiction up for consideration more quickly, you are moving along a process that the recipient is already legally charged with doing. These payments, if insubstantial, will not be an impediment to your moving forward. If the *facilitation fees* are to bribe a local official to do something that's illegal under local law, your organization would be violating the Foreign Corrupt Practices Act.[149]

Rural Health Clinic

Your nonprofit plans to donate critically needed medications to a foreign rural clinic that serves surrounding villages. The clinic has been operating for several years and has provided adequate data about its prior sources and uses of funds. The doctor who runs the clinic has described to the satisfaction of your board the past, present and anticipated future activities of the clinic.

The medications must be kept cold until they are administered, so your nonprofit also plans to donate funds to purchase a refrigerator for the clinic and a refrigerated truck to transport the medication to patients in the surrounding scattered villages. The doctor has an established track record; however in performing its pre-grant due diligence, your nonprofit becomes aware that certain local militia are very active on some of the routes the truck will need to travel, so there is no guarantee that the medications won't be diverted to purposes other than the purpose for which your grant was made. The name of the local militia group is not on the OFAC SDN list, but it is not possible to obtain names of the soldiers so they cannot be checked.

Do you proceed to donate the medications and funds?

To minimize the risk of diversion, your nonprofit might release supplies more frequently and in smaller amounts per shipment. It should also ask the doctor to provide more frequent quarterly or semiannual reports to you on the use of the funds and medications.

---

[149] For more about the Foreign Corrupt Practices Act of 1977, 15. U.S.C. §78dd-1, et seq., see **Chapter Eight**.

Jane Peebles, JD, TEP, ACTEC

Jane Peebles is a Senior Partner of Karlin & Peebles, LLP in Los Angeles. Her primary areas of practice are US and international estate and charitable planning. She represents high net worth families, entrepreneurs, philanthropists, and nonprofits. She is a frequent speaker and author on a variety of domestic and international estate and charitable planning topics including "Implications of the Anti-Terrorist Financing Rules for US Charities Making Grants Abroad," "Emerging Legal Issues in International Philanthropy," and "Here There Be Dragons: Navigating the Waters of Cross-Border Philanthropy."

Jane taught an extensive course in cross-border philanthropy for the Certified Specialist in Planned Giving program for fifteen years. She is a Fellow of the American College of Trust and Estate Counsel (ACTEC) and is certified by the California State Bar Association as a Specialist in Estate Planning, Probate, and Trust Law. Her peers have voted her a Southern California Super Lawyer every year since 2004 and a Best Lawyer in America in the Specialty of Trusts and Estates every year since 2008.

Chapter Ten

Monitoring and Impact Measurement

David Pritchard

Congratulations! You have not only decided to be an international grantmaker, but you have also successfully navigated the ethical, legal, and tax issues, identified the right tools for your giving, found and vetted the right charities to give to, and have given them grants. But while this may be the end of the giving process, it is only day one for the purpose of your giving—creating a positive impact in the world.

This chapter looks at how you can assess the difference your grants make to the lives of the intended beneficiaries. It does not provide detailed steps to fit your specific portfolio of grants. That requires a customized plan. Instead, this chapter provides the fundamentals and discusses the key challenges you are likely to face and advises you on how to address them. The guidance will help you navigate the complex work of measurement and impact assessment to avoid frustration and wasting precious resources.

There are five key points to bear in mind as you read this chapter (and afterward too!):

◆ Appropriate monitoring and impact measurement begins with clearly understanding the goals of your grantmaking, both your own organizational goals as well as the goals of the grants themselves. Below we discuss the *why* of measurement as well as how measurement fits into a broader plan-do-check-act cycle.

◆ It is not just your funding that can create positive change; *how you try to assess or measure that change* can also help. How? By using the monitoring and measurement activities to *promote learning and continuous improvement* for your grantees, not just to create numbers and stories to include in reports—though a good approach to monitoring and assessing impact will do both.

◆ You have choices to make about how you assess the impact of your grantmaking. There is not a one-size-fits-all approach. The main choice is between a simple approach that gives you approximate answers or a complicated one that gives you rigorous results. Unfortunately, an approach that is both simple and rigorous is rarely an option! This chapter gives guidance on the key choices you have to make.

> Two good sources of information on the evaluation and impact assessment practices of foundations are the Center for Effective Philanthropy's *Benchmarking Foundation Evaluation Practices*, and New Philanthropy Capital's *Funding an Impact*.

◆ Your ability to assess the impact of your grantmaking is *very dependent on the ability of grantees to assess their impact*. Your options and choices depend both on the type and depth of relationship you have with them (e.g., are you a hands-off grantmaker who has little interaction with your grantees other than providing financial support or are you more engaged and provide other forms of support?) as well as their capabilities. What you choose to do can possibly cause more harm than good if you place unnecessary requirements or unreasonable expectations on your grantees.

◆ Assessing the impact of your grants is not an exact science and will involve judgment and uncertainty. There are methods and tools that can help bring objectivity to the assessment, but do not expect *proof* of your impact. Another important choice for you will be whose judgments—primarily your grantees'—and which methods can you have confidence in.

Measuring Impact: What?

Once you have decided the goals to focus on measuring progress toward those goals might seem to simply be a question of collecting relevant data. But behind this apparent simplicity are a number of questions to answer first, such as:

◆ Who should decide what data is relevant and then collect and analyze it? Should you leave this to the grantee who might know best but be unintentionally or intentionally biased? Should you use an independent third party? Should you do some of this yourself or in collaboration with the grantee?

◆ How frequently should you assess progress toward the goals?

◆ How do you know any apparent progress toward the goals is due to the program and would not have happened anyway?

◆ How do you measure the impact of your grant to an organization or program if you are not the sole funder?

◆ How do you assess or aggregate the impact of multiple grants or an entire portfolio, not just individual grants?

The Terminology Challenge

The world of measurement, monitoring, and impact assessment can be confusing in part because of the terminology and the concepts. Some terms are used interchangeably, and experts sometimes define other terms in ways that are different from how they are used in everyday language. Even worse, some terms are defined by professional evaluators differently from how someone from the philanthropic or the financial sector defines them! For example, when an evaluator refers to a *significant impact* they are likely to mean an impact that is judged to have been caused by a program based on a statistical test. In everyday use, a significant impact often means a *large impact*.

This chapter uses the term *assessment* to refer to making a judgment about the effects of a grant or the grantee's program or services based on available information. Assessment is often a synonym for evaluation, but the latter sometimes carries with it an expectation of a formal methodology and level of rigor we don't assume in this chapter.

Measurement is used in the chapter to refer to both the act or result of measuring using a specific tool, such as a survey, as well as a synonym for both assessment and evaluation, as described above. It is clear from the context which applies.

A good source of other definitions and explanations of any differences is the Impact Management Project glossary which can be found on the website of Social Value US.

Answering these questions involves making choices, as noted above. One determining factor is why you want to assess the impact of your grantmaking in the first place. Below we discuss this as well as the main options you have and how to go about making the right choices to suit your grantmaking.

Before we get to that, let's start by getting some important concepts clear.

What Do We Mean by Impact (and Other Important Concepts)?

Impact refers to the difference that a program or service makes to the lives of the participants and other stakeholders. This seems simple enough. But the term can be problematic because it is typically used in one of two ways and it is not always clear from the context which is meant:

1. The broad definition covers all apparent effects of a program including those that are unintended as well as intended, long term and short term, direct and indirect, and measured or not measured.

2. The narrow definition refers to the short and/or long-term effects of a program as measured by *a rigorous assessment of the counter-factual*—an estimate of what would likely have happened if not for the program—typically using a control group or compara-tor group. This narrow definition entails a strong statement that says, if it were not for this program, this impact would not have happened.

The difference in the meaning boils down to the scope of the effects and whether the effects were measured using a counterfactual to give a rigor-ous result. The different meanings can create ambiguity and confusion. For example, if you ask nonprofits about the impact of their educational programs, you might get different answers. One might compare reading scores of participants with those of a comparator group, another might talk more broadly about the effect of the program on the lives of students, family members, and the communities where the program operates. A third answer might combine both. None of these are right or wrong in terms of what they mean by impact, but they have different emphases and implications about the rigor of the approach used.

We don't advocate one definition over another, but you and your grant-ees will have to choose: how broad should the assessment be (i.e., do you only measure the effects on direct beneficiaries or do you include other downstream effects on, for example, families and the community, etc.) and how rigorous should the assessment methodology be? *Typically, the broader the effects you want to measure and the more rigorous the methodology, the more it costs to assess the impact.*

The Counterfactual, Control, and Comparator Groups

The counterfactual is our best guess at what the world would be like in the absence of the program that is being assessed. The problem with the counterfactual is its hypothetical character—we have to create a world where the program we are assessing does not exist. Such a world can only be estimated, not measured. There are various ways to estimate the counterfactual; using a control group or a comparator group is one.

A control group is a group of people who are randomly selected to *not* receive the services of the program being evaluated. A common use of a control group is to test medicines, when the control group is given a placebo. The same approach can be used to test the effectiveness of social programs. The control group is tracked alongside the program participants, and the relevant differences between the two groups are an estimate of the impact of the program. The random selection is important as it allows the evaluator to estimate whether any differences between the participating group and the control group are likely to be the result of chance or the effect of the program.

A comparator group is similar to a control group in that it does not receive the services of the program but is chosen in some other way, such as being very similar to the participant group, rather than randomly.

Many evaluators like control groups or comparator groups even though they are typically costly because they provide a rigorous and objective assessment of a program's impact. Other ways of estimating the counterfactual, such as relying on the reports of beneficiaries as to what they think would have happened if not for the program, or assuming the situation before the program started would not have changed, are usually more subjective and susceptible to bias or errors. But nonprofits and their funders typically find these other ways acceptable given the cost of more rigorous approaches. This is a classic example of the choice between cost and rigor.

Keep in mind that grantees can only do what their funders provide resources for. If you and other funders want a broad and very rigorous assessment, collectively you will have to help fund this.

Qualitative and Quantitative Data

Another choice you and your grantees will have to make is whether to use *qualitative data*—i.e., non-numeric information that describes qualities or characteristics rather than quantities or measured values—or *quantitative data*—information that can be expressed as numbers—or both, to assess the impact of your grants.

The best choice largely depends on the nature of the program. Some impacts, such as reading test scores or incidence of disease, can often be easily measured quantitatively, while others, such as women's empowerment and human rights, are not. Also, remember that quantitative measures are approximations and simplifications of the impact. For example, the impact of an educational program is not captured fully, and some might argue not mostly, in improved test scores.

Numbers are useful because they provide a sense of scale of change (e.g., how many people affected) and the degree of change that qualitative data, such as stories and case studies, typically do not do. Numbers are also easy to grasp for stakeholders who are not familiar with the nature of the program, and so are useful for reporting. In contrast, qualitative data provides a richer understanding of the impact of the program and is often easier for people to relate to at a human level.

As there are benefits to both quantitative and qualitative data, good practice is to combine them. This has the added benefit of helping to *triangulate* data; that is, use data from multiple sources to validate each other. Think of assessing impact as putting together a jigsaw, where each data element—quantitative or qualitative—is a piece that when joined together help to show the impact of the grant. You do not need every piece of data to get a good idea of the impact, but it helps to have good quality data of different types.

Attribution and Contribution

So far, we have discussed what we mean by the impact of the program and what type of data we can use to assess impact. But as a funder, you probably want to know more than whether the *program* made a difference. You might want to know whether your *grant* made a difference.

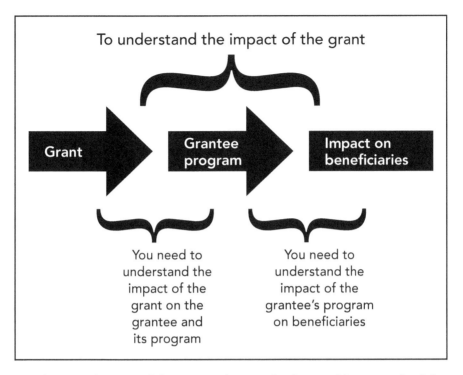

In other words, you might want to know whether and how much of the impact can be *attributed* to your grant. In fact, you face two attribution challenges. First, can any apparent impact be attributed to the grantee program as opposed to something else that is going on? Secondly, can the effectiveness of the program be attributed to your funding?

In both cases, attribution is usually tricky, because, as discussed above, we can never be really sure of what would happen if not for the program or the grant. The use of control groups and comparator groups can help understand the counterfactual and thus help attribute apparent impacts to the grantee's program rather than other causes. But there are other options. For example, interviews with stakeholders, especially beneficiaries of the program, can also shed light on whether it was the program that made the difference. Attributing changes to a program involves ruling out alternative explanations. This is a complex process, but the most important element is to have an inquisitive and open mind and encourage your grantees to do the same.[150]

---

[150] For a useful source see the section on Understand Causes on the Better Evaluation website, *betterevaluation.org/en/plan/understandcauses*.

It is unlikely you are the only funder of a program, and less likely the only funder of your grantee. Assuming that the grantee program has an impact that can be measured, and you are one of several funders, how do you separate out the impact of your grant?

There are two broad options:

1. You can describe, qualitatively, your contribution to the grantee and its programs, noting that creating impact is a collective effort and it is not meaningful to try to attribute parts of the impact to different parties and funders.

2. You can calculate, quantitatively, your contribution as the portion of total funding, and use that as an estimate of how much impact to attribute to your grant.

The second option appeals to those who really want to be able to describe the impact of their funding in quantitative terms. But many find this option does not reflect reality. For example, if you provide 25 percent of the funding for an organization that helps 1,000 people a year, do you help 250 people or 1,000 people? Is such a distinction meaningful?

It is naturally tempting to want to find out *exactly* how your grant helped, and there are ways it can be done in some situations. But these tend to be costly because they are rigorous and require specialized skills, and even then, embarking on such a quest may be fruitless. For this reason, many evaluators prefer to talk about an organization's *contribution* to the change they are pursuing, rather than attributing a program or a grant to a specific change.

Whichever you choose, the question of why you might want to be able to point to the specific difference your grant made turns out to be important, so let us consider that next.

Why Measure Impact?

There are three broad reasons why you want to measure the impact of your grantmaking:

◆ To *prove* to yourself and your stakeholders that you (as a funder) have made a difference

◆ To *improve or learn*, so you can make a bigger difference in the future

◆ To *build knowledge* so that others can learn as well

Most grantmakers, whether corporate or foundations, are interested in all three to some degree or other. But the relative weight you give to each will affect your choices for how you assess the impact. Most notably, if your main interest is reporting to your stakeholders about the difference your grants make, you are likely to prefer an approach that is simple, inexpensive, and provides approximate results, based on important information your grantee provides. It may not be necessary to be very rigorous. But if you want to help your grantee improve their program and create evidence for others to use, rigor may be more important.

The desire to aggregate impacts of different grants is mainly related to the first reason, to simply demonstrate the effect of your funding to stakeholders. In theory, being able to aggregate impacts implies you can also distinguish the contribution of each grant to the overall impact. But aggregating impacts requires a common measure of impact across grants, such as the number of people affected by the grants or monetary value of the impact. In practice, this is often impossible or difficult.[151] Even when it is possible, it typically involves losing details that are important for the second and third reasons given above. So there is often a trade-off between the simplicity of an aggregate measure and the meaningfulness of the impact measures. For example, knowing that all your grants helped five-thousand people does not tell you in what ways and by how much they helped. Knowing which of the three reasons are most important to you will help you make this trade-off between a single aggregate measure and the meaningfulness of the impact measures.

The "why" of measuring impact will also affect if and how to report results. For example, if your main aim is to demonstrate the difference you have made to stakeholders such as to employees, shareholders, or trustees, you are likely to want to emphasize the main positive effects and leave out details. When you want to learn and help others to learn, including your grantee, you should, however, include both what worked well and potential for improvements at whatever level of detail is needed.

Who Measures?

So far we have mainly talked about measuring impact as if this is something that you will be doing as a funder. But rarely will you actually be doing the measurement or evaluation yourself. Mostly it will be done

---

[151] For a discussion on when converting impacts into monetary figures is a good idea, see: Marina Svistak and David Pritchard, *Economic Evaluation: What is it good for?* (London: New Philanthropy Capital, 2014).

by the grantees themselves, or in some cases a third party, such as an independent evaluator.

This is where the question of judgment and capability is important. Does your grantee have appropriate skills, incentives, and experience, to assess their impact using appropriate methods so that you can have confidence in the results? If the answer is *yes*, that is great. Your role is to use the data and assessment they provide and make sure they retain that capability. If the answer is *no*, you have two choices: either find some-one else—such as a professional evaluator—to assess, or build up the internal measurement and evaluation capabilities of your grantee. The latter will not happen overnight so is probably best considered when you are making a medium or long-term commitment to a grantee.

In reality, the answer is unlikely to be a straight yes or no and will depend on the nature of the organization and their programs. International nonprofits might have a dedicated measurement and evaluation team, whereas small, local, charities may only have a handful of staff in total and little capacity or knowledge to assess their impact.

In such cases, your role as a funder will differ based on your grantees' capabilities and your relationship with them, although the guidance in this chapter is relevant in all cases. For more experienced grantees you will mostly be a consumer of information they provide. Your role will be to engage with them constructively to make sure you understand how they evaluate their work, what challenges they face in doing so, and how they address them. For grantees who do not have the necessary capa-bilities, you will need to match your requests with their capabilities, help them improve their capabilities, and bring in third parties to make assessments if appropriate.

When Should You Measure?

The appropriate timing of assessment depends on several factors:

◆ The timing of the program (e.g., is it a continuous service such as health care, or does it have a cycle, such as children's education)

◆ The pace of change brought about by program (e.g., do the changes take years to become apparent, such as some environ-mental improvements, or are they immediately observable)

◆ Your funding cycle (e.g., do you review grants annually, bi-annually, or other?)

◆ Your grantees' management and reporting cycle; It helps if your reporting needs fit with their cycle rather than the other way around. They likely have other funders they have to report to, and being out of sync with their practices is one way that your practices might hinder, rather than help the assessment practices

◆ The rigor and depth of the assessment

For all these points there is an important distinction between monitoring and evaluation. Monitoring is the periodic tracking to make sure an intervention is running as intended, whereas evaluation is an assessment of the difference the intervention makes. Monitoring takes place more frequently than an evaluation but does not look as closely as to whether the program has the intended effect. There is no fixed rule as to when either monitoring or evaluation should take place; the points above apply. The important point is the choices need to be theoretically and practically appropriate.

The issue of timing of assessment is relevant because it highlights that making an impact is not a one-time event but happens over time. For that and other reasons, it is useful to think about measuring impact as part of a cycle.

The Planning, Measurement, and Evaluation Cycle

Just as transferring grants is not the end of your job as a grantmaker, making an assessment of your grant's impact is not the end of the assessment process. Indeed, it is neither the end nor the beginning, but the middle of an ongoing planning and evaluation cycle. Thinking of assessing impact as part of a cycle, rather than a one-time event, is useful because it helps keep the purpose of assessment at the forefront of the choices you have to make. This will help ensure that you make appropriate choices and do not waste your and your grantees' time and resources.

We suggest the Plan-Do-Check-Act (or PDCA) cycle. This is a well-known management tool, and there are many variations used in the private, public, and nonprofit sectors. In the world of grantmaking, measurement and evaluation make up the *check* step in the PDCA cycle, although in practice using this cycle is not a set of four linear steps where one ends and the other begins, but rather all four overlap.

The cycle describes the broader decision-making process that involves what issues to focus on, choosing grantees, and the role that you want to play (e.g., are you only a funder or will you provide other support?). The idea is that creating a positive impact is best thought of as a deliberative activity where you want to get the most from, and help others get the most from, your grant. Typically, the better informed you are as a grant-maker, the greater impact you are likely to have.

Plan

As noted above, one of the first steps in assessing the impact of your grantmaking is to be clear on what the goals of the grants are in the first place. You don't want to be comparing actual vs. intended if you aren't clear on what is intended![152]

As this chapter is about assessing impact, we do not cover the question of how to decide what to focus on. There is other guidance on this,[153] and you might want to revisit **Chapter Two** on the Sustainable Development Goals (SDGs). Just a word of caution. Some impacts are easier to measure than others. It might be tempting to focus your grantmaking where you can most easily assess the impact. But *being easy to measure is not the same thing as important or effective*! Your most effective grants might be those that are hardest to measure the impact of because their effects are wide-ranging and long-term.

Choosing what issues you want to tackle and organizations you want to support are not the only decisions to make in the planning stage. This is the time to also decide what data you will need to assess the impact of your grants. Don't wait until after you have made the grants.

In some cases, you can choose to use a predefined framework and/or method to assess the impact of your grant. There is a range of frameworks and methods to choose from.[154] Frameworks generally identify what to measure, and methods generally explain how to measure, but there is often overlap between these. They have the advantage of being off-the-shelf, and so the work of deciding what to measure or how to

---

[152] The evaluation of the DARE (Drug Abuse Resistance Education) program is a well-known case of the problem of assessing the effects of a program against the stated goals rather than goals that stakeholders valued. *See* Sarah Birkeland, Erin Murphy-Graham, and Carol Weis. "Good reasons for ignoring good evaluation: The case of the drug abuse resistance education (DARE) program," *Evaluation and Program Planning*, 28, 247-256, 2005.

[153] For example, see: Angela Kail, and David Plimmer, *Theory of Change for Funders: Planning to make a difference.* (London: New Philanthropy Capital, 2014.)

[154] You can find different frameworks and methods on the Better Evaluation website, and the Foundation Center's Tools and Resources for Assessing Social Impact (TRASI).

measure is already done, more or less. An example of a predefined framework is the World Health Organization Quality of Life (WHOQOL) assessment tool. An example method is the *Most Significant Change* method which involves generating and analyzing personal accounts of change from beneficiaries and deciding which of these accounts is the most significant and why.

The problem with using predetermined frameworks and methods is that finding ones that are relevant may take some time, even ones you do find might not be completely suitable for the programs you fund, and, probably most importantly, it is likely to be unhelpful and possibly counterproductive for you as a funder to push a particular framework or method on a grantee. The exception to this is if they do not have capacity to do this themselves, in which case your advice is helpful. But if they do not have the capacity to find appropriate frameworks or methods you might also be concerned about their capacity to use ones that you find.

In the absence of a ready-made and appropriate framework, a widely used approach for identifying what data you might need is to start with a Theory of Change.[155] A Theory of Change is simply a way of describing how the program activities are expected to bring about the intended impact. It spells out the causal links between activities, intermediate or short-term outcomes, and final or longer-term goals. You can collect data, both qualitative and quantitative, to help assess whether that logical sequence is happening in fact, not just in theory.

While many find a Theory of Change as a useful tool for planning and evaluation, it does have potential drawbacks. The first is that it focuses attention on intended and positive impacts and as a consequence, you and your grantees may ignore any unintended and negative impacts of the program. The second is it carries the risk of locking an organization into one approach rather than being adaptable to change.

If you do decide to use a Theory of Change to help assess the impact of your grants, make sure that it fits with your grantees' understanding of the impact they think, or intend, to have.

Do

For you as a grantmaker, this step refers to the process of making grants which is covered by the rest of this book. Just to emphasize a point made above, if you are expecting grantees to provide you with data on their

---

[155] Kail and Plimmer, 2014.

impact, you need to provide resources to help them do this. Being clear on what you expect and are willing to fund will go a long way in helping your grantees become learning organizations and use data efficiently, rather than just collect data simply to report to you and other funders.

Check

This step in the cycle covers both monitoring and evaluation as a check as to whether what was intended—both how the program is being implemented and the planned effects—are actually occurring.

As discussed above, to do this you will mostly be checking by reviewing data and information provided by someone else, typically the grantee, but possibly by a third party evaluator. By necessity, your grantees will have to be selective about what they measure and report. Depending on your relationship with them and the types of data and method(s) you and/or they have chosen, you may or may not know how they have decided what to measure and report.

In either case, you should consider four potential *filters* that affect how the underlying impact of the grantee will appear to you as the reviewer:

◆ Framing: What is included and excluded from the data and report?

◆ Methods: How does the report count, describe, estimate, and value the underlying impact?

◆ Presentation: How is the information about the impact presented in the report?

◆ Perspective: Whose perspective(s) does the report take, based on its purpose and audience?

Act

What you do with the knowledge you gain from checking the data depends on why you wanted to assess the impact of your grantmaking as discussed above. You might just use the information to report to your stakeholders, such as employees or the board, about the impact of the grants. Maybe the review leads to discussions with the grantee about how they can increase their impact and how you can support that, and internal discussions about how you can improve your grantmaking. Or maybe you decide to publish the findings so that others can use the information as well. Or possibly a mix of some or all of these.

Framework for Reviewing Impact Reporting

Social Value United States and Social Value Canada have developed a framework to help funders and other reviewers assess impacts reports. The framework includes questions that reviewers should consider to help them understand how well the report reflects the underlying impact that is the subject of the report. The questions are organized under three different lenses that affect what the reader of the report sees:

Framing:

◆ *Boundary*: What is the boundary of the entity being assessed? (Evaluators call this the evaluand.)

◆ *Scope*: Which subjects and issues are examined? Are indirect effects included?

◆ *Causal chain*: Which parts of the organization's operations are included (e.g., does the report include the effect of the organization's supply chain or just the effect of their services and products)?

◆ *Timeframe*: What is the time period of activity covered by the report? What is the timeframe of impacts in the report?

Methods:

◆ *Measurement*: How robust are the methods and trustworthy are the data used to count, describe or estimate outputs and outcomes?

◆ *Causality*: How do the chosen methods address causality and attribution? What is the level of certainty around causality?

◆ *Valuation*: What methods are used for valuing social impacts?

Presentation:

◆ *Depth of content*: How did the report writers decide how much detail to provide?

◆ *Neutrality*: Were the findings reported in a balanced way? Have any parts of the report been independently reviewed or assured?

◆ *Emphasis*: What was emphasized and de-emphasized in the report?

There is an additional meta-lens that affects each of these three lenses:

Perspective:

◆ *Audience*: Who is the target audience of the report?

◆ *Purpose*: What is the intended purpose of the report?

◆ *Stakeholder engagement*: Which stakeholders were consulted, and not consulted, in preparation of the report?

◆ *Authorship*: Who wrote the report, and do they have the right skills and experience?

Whichever you choose, by this point you have now gone beyond giving money to create a positive impact in the world to using the planning and evaluation cycle to make sure the impact increases over time.

David Pritchard

David Pritchard advises nonprofit, private, and public sector organizations on how to assess and increase their social impact. He supports effective change-makers by helping them plan and evaluate what they do. David has more than twenty-five years of experience working with government agencies, nonprofits, and foundations in the United Kingdom and the United States.

David teaches planning and evaluation methods at Adler University, Chicago. He was formerly an economist for New York City Economic Development Corporation and Head of Measurement and Evaluation at New Philanthropy Capital in London.

David has a BA degree from Oxford University, an MA in International Peace Studies from the University of Notre Dame, and an MBA from Yale University.

Chapter Eleven

Preparing for an Audit

Victoria Bjorklund

U S charitable organizations that engage in global grantmaking and/ or operations must expect to be audited. Thus, the leaders of those organizations should plan and execute their programs in anticipation of responding to audit requests. This chapter provides practical advice about how your organization can save money by constructing your operating procedures and files so that they will efficiently yield the necessary information when your organization is eventually audited. This chapter also provides an overview of how the audit process might be initiated, carried out, and closed.

Building an Efficient Record-Keeping System

An Audit of Some Kind Is Inevitable

US charitable organizations that engage in global grantmaking and/or operations never want to be audited. The reality, however, is that someday every global organization will be audited by someone, whether that someone is a US government agency like the Internal Revenue Service (IRS) or a state attorney general, a non-US government agency like the UK Charity Commission, an international organization, a funder (very common), or an internal audit authorized by the organization's board of directors. As a result, global grantmakers should organize their operations and their records to anticipate producing some or all of those records when an audit materializes.

What Is an Audit?

The word *audit* is defined by Merriam-Webster as "a formal examination of an organization's... accounts or financial situation" or "a methodical examination and review." Audits may be of financial accounts, or they may be of operations, files, policies, practices, or procedures. Often a funder will specify that the charitable organization must make periodic reports to the funder covering specific topics. Frequently, the funder will reserve the right in its grant-award contract to review the books and records underlying the reports it receives. Audits by independent certified public accountants may take place annually and follow "generally accepted accounting procedures" (GAAP). Sometimes organizations operating in more than one country will learn that these audits are subject to different rules in different parts of the world and that, for example, reconciling US financial reporting with European financial reporting may require extra work and conversations.

Finally, many people think of an audit by the IRS when they hear the word *audit*. An IRS audit is a particular kind of review. It can take any one of several forms. The IRS Tax-Exempt and Government Entities (TE/GE) Commissioner in the FY 2016 Priorities Letter stated that the Exempt Organizations Division's overarching strategy is to "ensure organizations enjoying tax-exempt status comply with the requirement for exemption and adhere to all applicable federal tax laws. This strategy will be implemented through data-driven decisions." The approaches to compliance identified by the Commissioner include:

◆ Educational efforts

◆ Compliance reviews

◆ Compliance checks

◆ Correspondence examinations, and

◆ Field examinations

While only correspondence examinations and field examinations may technically be *audits*, the word *audit* is used colloquially to refer to any kind of inquiry. Most of the rules I discuss below relate specifically to IRS audits, but some non-IRS auditors may follow or refer to IRS rules or practices.

The IRS Is Interested in International Grantmaking and Operations

The IRS Tax-Exempt and Government Entities (TE/GE) Commissioner in the FY 2016 Priorities Letter identified five key areas of IRS focus. The fourth of five topics was "International: Issues include oversight on funds spent outside the United States including funds spent on potential terrorist activities, exempt organizations operating as foreign conduits, and Report of Foreign Bank and Financial Accounts (FBAR) requirements, enforced through compliance reviews, compliance checks, correspondence audits, and field examinations." This Priorities Letter thus lists in the last sentence the different ways that the IRS might audit the international operations or grants of a US organization.

What Are the Mechanics of an IRS Examination?

The IRS revised its audit procedures effective April 1, 2017. Each of the approaches would be initiated by a letter specifying that the organization has been selected for review and stating the year or years involved, the name of the revenue agent, and the name and contact information of the revenue agent's supervisor. The initiation letter might also be accompanied by one or more "Information Document Requests" (each an IDR). When this initiation letter is received, it is important that you review it promptly and carefully to assess which kind of review is occurring and who you need to get involved. Make sure that you focus on when your reply is due. Compliance reviews and compliance checks are generally more limited in scope than correspondence audits and field examinations. Thus, those reviews and checks might be able to be handled in-house or by the organization's experienced return preparer or outside attorney. The individuals preparing the response to the IDR(s) must understand what each IDR is requesting, whether it is reasonable to gather and submit the required information and documents from the records kept by the organization, and appropriately articulate the organization's explanation of the facts contained in the documentation. If the organization has been selected for a correspondence audit or a field examination, the organization will likely wish to discuss the substance and procedures with outside counsel or the return preparer. Ideally, inside and outside persons will work as a team to present an accurate and clear telling of the organization's story, backed up by relevant documentation.

The best time to prepare for an audit is before one begins. Specifically, since some kind of audit is inevitable, your organization is well advised to plan ahead for the inevitable. I can't tell you how many times clients have thanked me for helping them organize their record keeping in a way that would make responding to an audit someday a feasible task. It's great when a client says to you, "We got an audit letter, and we're ready to answer it. You always warned us that this day would come and now it has, but we feel prepared." Even better is when the audit closes with a *no-change letter*, which in the case of an IRS audit means that no concerns were identified that would require any change in operations.

So long before an audit is initiated, what can an organization do to get ready? The answer is to follow policies and procedures that create precisely the documentation that the organization will have to produce upon audit. While one can never know precisely what will be requested, the *expenditure responsibility* regulations and the *control and discretion* revenue rulings both provide reliable road maps on the kind of information that would likely be requested. This is true even if the organization is a public charity not subject to the *expenditure responsibility* regulations. The thinking is that auditors would not likely require more reporting from a public charity than they would of a private foundation, the less-favored classification.

So by complying with the expenditure responsibility record-keeping requirements, all organizations should feel comfortable that they will be in the ballpark for having at hand the materials that would be responsive to IDRs and other forms of request. Of course, if a particular donor has contracted for additional or different information, be sure to collect and store that information from the beginning as well. Remember that it always costs less to set up an inclusive record-keeping system now before a project or operations begin than it will to try to gather and piece together information later.

What Action Steps Does This Advice Translate Into?

Organize Records in Real Time Before an Audit Materializes

Documents can be kept digitally in scanned form or in hard copy, or a combination of the two. Digital copies that can either be emailed or printed out if needed are generally preferred today.

Begin by making sure that the organization has digital copies of its organizing documents. Those include the organization's:

◆ Original certificate of incorporation or trust instrument,

◆ Any amendments to those originals,

◆ Original bylaws and any amendments, including resolutions,

◆ IRS Form 1023 and any correspondence about it with the IRS,

◆ The IRS determination letter, any subsequent IRS correspondence including correspondence about the end of an advance ruling period or any reclassification of public charity or private foundation classification,

◆ IRS Forms 990 or 990-PF for every year,

◆ Any state or local annual filings,

◆ Complete documentation of every IRS audit or inquiry, including any IDRs, replies to IDRs, and closing letters or settlement documents,

◆ Responses to any other audit, examination, review, or government registration or filing,

◆ Form 8940—Miscellaneous Determination Requests—if any,

◆ Private letter ruling requests and replies, if any,

◆ Accountable plan, convenience of the employer, or any other policies related to compensation or exclusion of amounts from compensation, and

◆ Rebuttable-presumption-of-reasonableness, related-party, or interested director approvals, including any background or appraiser reports and minutes approving the transactions.

Keep Contemporaneous Written Records of the Organization's Internal Operations (Especially the Following)

Documentation about the Composition of the US Board of Directors for Every Year

Is the organization's board in every year composed of directors who are US citizens or residents not acting on behalf of a foreign organization? Do the bylaws have a *US class* and a *non-US class,* with the US class always having at least one more director than the non-US class? Do the representatives of the foreign charity hold any voting privileges or restrictions that could give the foreign-charity directors undue power over decisions? Are the boards of the grantor and grantee organizations too similar?

See, e.g., Priv. Ltr. Rul. 91-29-040 (April 23, 1991), in which the IRS approved a *Friends of* organizational structure in which the organization had seven directors, three of whom had to be approved by the foreign charity and two of the three were required for a quorum and for amendment of the bylaws. This structure may represent the *outer limits* of IRS tolerance for overlapping board members representing the interests of the foreign charity or charities.

If your organization's structure goes this far or further, you will want to consider in advance how you would defend the structure as a governance matter and as an operations matter. To document operations, you would want to be able to produce records of how directors voted on grants and other financial matters. If your bylaws are in any way too permissive or unclear, consider amending them now to be sure that your organization would not fail on structural grounds.

Funding and Record-Keeping Procedures for Every Grant

Rev. Rul. 63-252 sets out expectations that US boards will exercise control and discretion over the approval, allocation, and stewardship of funds raised in the United States but expended outside the United States either directly or indirectly through grants to non-US organizations. Rev. Rul. 66-79 posits that projects were "previously reviewed and approved by the board of directors" before granted funds are transferred to the non-US recipient. The IRS expects the US organization to keep "contemporaneous written records." Your organization may wish to keep and refer to copies of these revenue rulings as you document the organization's compliance with them. Your organization will want to keep in *each grant file* at least excerpted minutes and/or resolutions that document the exercise of control and discretion over funds expended or granted. Your organization's file for each grant should document that your organization solicited or received unsolicited, reviewed, and pre-approved one or more projects before your organization starts soliciting funds in the United States for any project. Once US-sourced funds are received from donors, you should have your US board expressly approve a resolution approving the expenditure of those funds in a grant for the specified project as being in furtherance of the US organization's exempt purposes.

At the risk of repeating this point, keep in the grant file digital or hard copies of:

◆ The resolutions and/or meeting minutes pre-approving solicitation and then the resolutions and/or meeting minutes approving expenditure of every grant before it is sent out of the United States;

◆ Executed written grant-award agreements, including clauses limiting expenditure of the funds by the non-US grantee to the purposes agreed to and described in the pre-grant request and budget, which should be attached to the grant agreement, and also the requirement that the grantee report back to the US organization;

◆ Every written report back to the US organization until the funds are expended in full or, if, the funder is a public charity, until the funder is confident that the grant funds have been used in accordance with the grant terms and are safe from diversion. If the US organization had to request return or reallocation of granted funds, be sure to keep in the grant file those records too.

On audit, my clients have had auditors look at reports from the non-US grantees to see if the reports contain evidence that they were read by the US organization's staff (e.g., reviewer's notes or highlighting) or otherwise marked as reviewed by the recipient US organization. Employers should remind their staff members to pay attention to the accuracy and tone of any notes they may write on reports as they may later be asked to explain what they wrote and what follow-up action they took, if any.

I recommend that your US organization create a checklist for each grant so that you are sure that each file contains the required documents. I also recommend that your US organization create and use for approving every grant a form resolution that contains the expected language about the grant being in furtherance of the US organization's exempt purposes. By following these steps as your grants are planned and executed, you will simplify and conform your record keeping to what you will actually need on audit.

Read and Learn from Other Organizations' Experiences

As a practical matter, nothing is more informative than reading about another organization's audit experiences and learning from its mistakes. Because the IRS does not discuss audits publicly, I start by looking each year at the IRS Annual Plan and its identification of what topics the IRS will be focusing on. I also look for the outcomes of prior year's audits. These typically take the form of reports IRS officials give in speeches or in various reports. Finally, I look whenever possible at revocation rulings and subsequent litigation, if any.

Revocation letters have become surprisingly easy to find by using an online search engine. These letters can be very informative to read. Let me give you a few relevant examples. To better help you understand what kind of records IRS auditors might wish to review, I recommend that you do a search online and read LTR 201511033 (March 15, 2015). This letter contains a final adverse determination by the IRS revoking exemption of a *Friends of* organization because the IRS determined that a more than insubstantial part of the organization's activities are not in furtherance of exempt purposes. As a result, the organization was found to have failed the "operated" half of the *organized and operated exclusively for exempt purposes* test set out in Treas. Reg. section 1.501(c)(3)-1(a)(1).

The IRS also proffered a secondary rationale for its actions: contributions to the organization are not deductible because the *Friends of* organization failed to exercise control and discretion over donated funds, with the result that the organization was operated as a *conduit* to a foreign organization not eligible to accept contributions deductible by US taxpayers who itemize deductions. The letter also explains that when the organization failed to respond to requests for information, the IRS Area Office sought the help of the IRS's Foreign Tax Attaché. The Foreign Tax Attaché, in turn, contacted the foreign country's taxing authority and the two conducted a collateral investigation.

The IRS letter explains the law, regulations, and anti-conduit authorities in some useful detail. The ruling also illustrates how the IRS applies the anti-conduit *control-and-discretion tests* to the facts at hand. In the present case, the IRS asserted that the *Friends of* organization was not operated for an exempt purpose because it did not maintain appropriate records showing, among other things, how specific grants were to be and were actually used. The IRS further stated that the "organization made other questionable payments and transactions totaling 50% of distributions for which no substantiation was provided to establish whether funds were used" for qualifying purposes.

Finally, the organization failed to establish that it maintained contemporaneous written records to verify that it exercised the required *control and discretion* over the funds it granted. Importantly, the IRS stated that the payment made to the foreign organization was "not for specific projects, but for the general operating expenses" of the foreign organization. Later in the letter, the IRS found that the organization "did not establish that it funded specific projects reviewed in advance" as required by the two seminal anti-conduit revenue rulings. Based on these findings, the IRS concluded that the *Friends of* organization acted as a conduit to the foreign organization "in effect making [the foreign organization] the actual donee organization." This letter is evidence that the anti-conduit rules are alive and well. Specifically, it shows how important it is for *Friends of* organizations to keep accurate and thorough and contemporaneous records of every grant request, every pre-approval, every written grant agreement, and every report back to document that the *Friends of* organization knows how funds will be spent before sending grants over borders and then gets reports back on whether the funds were spent as expected and not diverted.

To the best of my knowledge, this revocation letter is the first time that the IRS has published the government's view of problems inherent in paying general operating support without first reviewing and pre-approving the specific components of that support. This problem is easily avoidable by your organization. Doing so requires writing good documentation and executing good grantmaking procedures. If only the *Friends of* organization board of directors had pre-approved and in their grants enumerated approved components of general operating support—e.g., rent, utilities, teacher salaries and fringe benefits, maintenance-worker salaries and fringe benefits, etc.—the organization could likely have significantly improved its position on audit.

Lest you think that LTR 201511033 is an isolated example, see also LTR 201403018 (Jan. 17, 2014). In that revocation letter, the IRS ruled that an organization formed to support advanced Talmudic scholarship abroad did not qualify for tax-exempt status because its net earnings inured to the benefit of insiders and it lacked control and discretion over funds sent outside the United States. If you search and read that letter online, you will see another set of facts again showing you how not to run an organization. I believe that the IRS auditors were correct in their determinations in both cases because the US organizations were not able to produce the expected documentation.

Engaging Outside Attorneys and Accountants and Controlling Costs

When your organization receives notice of an audit, you will want to alert the appropriate officers and/or board members (e.g., the chairs of the audit committee and the finance committee). You will also want to consider the potential costs of the audit and how they will be funded.

Costs vary depending on which kind of review is initiated: a compliance review, a compliance check, a correspondence audit, or a field examination.

Most Costly Option

Of these four options, the field examination will likely be the most costly because it is likely to be wider in scope, may require production of more documents responsive to more IDRs, and may require more people inside and outside the organization to work on preparing written responses to IDRs.

Complex Audits Require Complex Record Keeping

They may also require legal counsel's attention to identifying and redacting privileged documents. If this is the case, legal counsel—inside or outside—should prepare a privilege log, an action that will lead to additional costs. Also, it sometimes becomes evident at the initiating meeting that the concerns are very serious and will involve numerous IDRs. If so, that is the time to "call in the cavalry" of the experienced advisors who can manage a complex document production operation.

For example, the organization should ask that every document request, even if previewed by phone, be reduced to writing in an IDR. IDRs will be numbered sequentially. Each response should include a copy of the IDR, and the response should be numbered in a manner that correlates with the IDR. If the IDR when received appears to be overly broad, the person representing the organization should negotiate with the revenue agent to narrow the scope. For example, instead of providing a copy of every scholarship award, the representative might ask if the IRS would accept a sampling of every eighth scholarship award in the year under audit.

We have had good results in narrowing the scope of overly broad IDRs by explaining to the agent why a full-scale response would be expensive, disruptive, redundant, or whatever the case might be. We have also had good results in obtaining extensions of time in which to respond or in working around busy times such as the organization's annual gala or the filing of its Form 990. Finally, we have found it useful in a complex audit to Bates-stamp every response. This helped outside counsel in preparing cross-references to earlier IDR responses in later IDR responses.

While helpful, this level of detail does add to costs but also aids outcomes. Also, if the IDR sets a return date that is too difficult for the organization to meet, speak with or email the revenue agent requesting an extension of time in which to respond. Generally, the revenue agent will be willing to provide a reasonable extension of time. If not, you can appeal to the agent's supervisor on this or other matters.

Finally, your organization may need legal help to determine whether any part of the documentation you might produce is in fact protected from production as privileged. This could include attorney-client communications. For this reason, your organization might need inside or outside counsel to review document production before submission to redact privileged text and to create a privilege log.

Applying for Technical Advice if Needed

If the audit agent is pursuing a negative path in an IRS audit on a subject that you believe should yield a favorable outcome for your organization, you may find yourself in a challenging situation. First, try to show the agent the merits of your organization's position, telling the story clearly and compellingly with emphasis on how the organization's actions comply with the law. If you are still unsuccessful, ask to speak with the audit agent's supervisor. You should know the identity of the supervisor from the initiating paperwork. If you discover that the supervisor shares the agent's negative view, ask the agent to *write up* their proposed position.

If possible, try again to make your best case. If all of these steps are unsuccessful, you might then find yourself in the position of having to apply for technical advice. In such an instance, the agent and the taxpayer's representative each write up their respective positions and submit them for technical advice. A decision is rendered, sometimes written up in a technical advice memorandum, so that the particular issue can be resolved and the audit can continue with this guidance in hand. If the guidance continues to be negative, then filing an internal appeal with the Appeals Division or going to court may be the organization's only option. My personal experience has generally been good when the channels of communication have been kept open with the agent and the agent's supervisor.

Where your organization clearly did something wrong, I have found that it is best proactively to adopt improved policies and procedures that will prevent the unwanted actions in the future and to be open about the constructive response taken proactively by the organization. Remember that in charity land the common goal is to have a charitable organization firing on all cylinders exclusively to advance its charitable mission. Therefore, getting the organization's house in order so that it can properly be mission-driven is typically the common goal between organization and agent.

For an overview of the audit process, including conducting meetings with the IRS, the three kinds of revenue agents and the significance of their participation, see the Charity and Security Network (CSN) Webinar entitled "IRS Audits of Nonprofits: How to Avoid or Prepare" (May 8, 2017), available online through CSN.

Victoria Bjorklund

Victoria B. Bjorklund is a Retired Partner at Simpson Thacher & Bartlett LLP where she founded and headed the Firm's Exempt Organizations Group.

Since 1989, Victoria has served as a director, *pro bono* legal counsel, and currently chairs the Board of Advisors for Doctors Without Borders. She is also a director of the Robin Hood Foundation, the Friends of Fondation de France, the Institute for Advanced Study in Princeton, Nutrition Science Initiative (NuSI), and the Lawyers' Committee for Civil Rights Under Law. Until recently, she was a trustee of the American Friends of the Louvre, the Louvre Endowment, and Princeton University.

Victoria is a former chair of the ABA Tax Section Committee on Exempt Organizations and of its subcommittee on International Philanthropy. She is the coauthor of *New York Nonprofit Law and Practice* (LexisNexis, 3d Ed. 2015) and annual supplements. She also taught The Law of Nonprofit Organizations at Harvard Law School for eight years ending in 2017.

She earned her JD at Columbia University School of Law, a PhD in Medieval Studies from Yale University, and a BA, *magna cum laude,* from Princeton University, where she graduated in three years and was elected to Phi Beta Kappa.

Chapter Twelve: Donor Perspectives

Part One: High Net Worth Individuals and Families as Global Donors

Susan Winer and Betsy Brill

Historically the United States has been the most philanthropic nation in the world. One reason for this may be the fact that there are tax advantages for high net worth individuals and families (HNW) who can use charitable donations to offset taxes on income and capital gains. But the charitable nature of Americans predates tax laws and is very much a part of the country's DNA.

The times they are a-changin', to paraphrase Bob Dylan, as the number of millionaires and billionaires around the world increases. There is a growing understanding within the global HNW population that with great wealth comes great responsibility and an opportunity to harness this wealth for good.

The question of multi-generational families "having enough money" is not solely a US issue, nor is the desire to acknowledge, act upon, and transfer generationally a sense of social responsibility. In light of the growing wealth globally, donors, nonprofits, and advisors alike want to better understand how to most effectively reach the most marginalized populations and solve our most protracted social and environmental issues.

To achieve impact and real change, we must *demystify* and *demythologize* what it takes to be an effective actor in the global landscape. Most charitable giving, particularly global, is not well planned or executed, leaving many donors with a level of dissatisfaction and lack of real confidence around the impact they are making with their charitable giving. Good practice on the part of all stakeholders will add real and necessary capital.

In this section, we explore the frameworks that HNW need to put in place to become effective global donors. We address the questions donors need to answer; the road map they need to establish to successfully engage current and future generations/stakeholders; the tools they have available in their philanthropic toolbox; and the elements of effective cross-border giving.

The Role of Advisors in Good Philanthropic Practice

HNW most often begin their philanthropic journey in the office of their trusted advisor—their estate planning attorney, financial or wealth advisor. HNW want to have the philanthropic conversation with their advisor(s), beyond just the transactional aspect. They would like to have their advisor initiate that conversation, or at the very least, make it a welcome part of discussions around investment of funds, estate planning, and transfer of wealth.

The initial conversation about philanthropy provides the baseline for good decision-making about vehicle choice, purpose, time horizon, and execution of the strategic plan that will influence the success of their philanthropic endeavors. An important part of the conversation is what the capacity for giving can be—whether during life or as part of the donor's legacy. Many people do not know what their capacity is or which assets they should be using to fulfill their charitable intent. Another consideration for donors is whether or not to give as much away as possible to *change the world* today and not to keep their wealth in their endowments or portfolios. This time horizon decision will influence asset allocation and how an investment portfolio is structured.

A good time to start a conversation with your clients is when there is a *trigger event*. For example:

◆ Death in the family

◆ Liquidity event

◆ Inheritance

◆ Divorce

◆ Rethinking goals for second half of life

As part of the conversation with a client, it is important to determine which vehicle is most appropriate for the donor. The responses to the

Some initial discussion points to incorporate into your conversations with clients:

Financial Distribution

◆ Do they fully understand their net worth, the source(s) of their funds, and the amount that would be (or could be) available for annual giving?

◆ How much money would they like to designate for charitable giving during their lifetime?

◆ If they are creating a giving vehicle, particularly a foundation, do they expect it to spend assets down over a limited period of time or last in perpetuity?

Defining Intent

◆ Does their current estate plan incorporate philanthropic wishes?

◆ Do the executor or heirs have the information they need to make decisions regarding where and how to distribute the philanthropic resources?

◆ How would they like to be remembered? What kind of *legacy* do they want to leave?

◆ Do they want their giving to occur primarily during their lifetime or after death?

◆ What, if any, is the geographic focus of their giving?

Deepening Philanthropic Engagement

◆ Have they thought about the issue areas in which they hope to effect change or the types of organizations to which they would like to give?

◆ How do they assess philanthropic opportunities?

◆ If they wanted to increase their giving, if only to avoid taxes, would they know where to give? Would they feel confident in those donations?

◆ Given their other commitments, how much time and involvement do they want to devote to their philanthropic endeavors?

Engaging the Next Generation

◆ Do they want to include their family in philanthropic decisions and activities?

◆ What values would they like to pass on to their children, grandchildren, and/ or significant others?

◆ Have they discussed their charitable interests, plans, and activities with family members?

◆ Have their family members been involved in any of the charitable giving decisions thus far?

◆ Have they faced any challenges involving the next generation in their philanthropy? Does the next generation have a different approach to philanthropy?

◆ Does the next generation want to participate in the family's philanthropy?

previous questions will help with this process. However, this may also be a suitable time to consider engaging a philanthropic advisor to work with you and your clients, particularly if your clients are seeking specific information or direction around a variety of philanthropic topics, questions, or challenges that you, as an advisor, may not feel knowledgeable or comfortable addressing.

A philanthropic advisor will be able to provide nuanced guidance around such issues as:

◆ Options for establishing a giving vehicle: how they are utilized as standalone vehicles or in combination

◆ Time horizon determination for a giving vehicle (spend-down or perpetuity)

◆ Evaluating past and current giving to determine degree of impact and alignment with interests and intent

◆ Identifying, assessing, and vetting interest areas and organizations to support

◆ Creating a mission statement

◆ Engaging the next generation in philanthropy

◆ Determining staffing needs to support giving

◆ Creating or formalizing a company's charitable giving as a business and marketing tool

◆ Researching international giving opportunities and recommending how best to implement them

◆ Ensuring the success of a major donation

What Donors Should Think About

As a thoughtful donor, your client wants to maximize the impact of their philanthropy. You can help make this happen, by discussing a few key components they can build into their philanthropy.

Too often an important step in the overall giving process is overlooked—establishing a solid framework for giving. Whether giving locally, globally, or some combination thereof, it is critical to clearly articulate focus and its construct. This framework is most often captured in a mis-

Key Aspects to Be Considered by Donors

◆ First: Clearly articulated interests, concerns and/or passions

◆ Second: A client-centered team that includes financial, legal, and philanthropic advisors

◆ Third: Responsiveness to community and organizational needs and the partnership between them and the grantee

◆ Fourth: The structure of gifts and the tax and financial implications

◆ Fifth: Understanding and applying best practices in the field

◆ Sixth: Clear and consistent communication between the donor and the grantee regarding priorities, processes and desired outcomes

◆ Seventh: Evaluation of the impact of gifts to ensure they adhere to your client's intent

Excerpted from *The Charitable Planning Desk Reference® for Advisors 4th Edition.* © Strategic Philanthropy, Ltd. 2017-2018.

sion statement. A mission statement defines what the donor is seeking to accomplish for whom and where. While often aspirational, it should also maintain a level of practicality, as it will guide the giving and serve as the touchpoint for gauging whether or not the giving is aligned with intent and the kind of impact that has been achieved.

The question of impact is always on donors' minds—how do I know I made a difference? Is there more that I can do? How can I leverage my philanthropic dollars? While impact may be on the mind of donors, defining it and achieving it are not always easy tasks. Take, as an example, the family that was adding members of the next generation to the family's foundation board. In trying to share family history, they realized their giving was reactive, not focused and proactive. There was no connection between issue areas, populations, or geography. They could neither share what had been accomplished with their philanthropy nor set the tone for expectations.

At the suggestion of their wealth advisor, the philanthropic family sought professional guidance to help them to create a mission statement and a framework for giving that represented the perspectives of all of the family members. This step allowed them to collectively measure the impact of their giving against the established framework.

Here are some of the questions that were asked of the donor:

◆ During your lifetime, what would you like to change in the world through your philanthropy?

◆ What broad areas or populations do you as philanthropic foundation envision supporting?

◆ What will it take to create this change?

◆ What kinds of organizations can help bring about these changes (If you are trying to mitigate the spread of a disease, do you look to fund universities, community-based health centers, or grassroots organizations that engage local communities to disseminate health information?)

◆ Have you considered partnering with others who are funding this work? Do you know how to find these funders? Are there gaps your philanthropy can fill to complement what others are doing?

◆ What due diligence is needed to ensure that you will be creating a successful and meaningful partnership that benefits all stakeholders?

Philanthropic Strategies

There are a variety of strategies donors can incorporate to accomplish their intended goals—from writing a check to a nonprofit to investing in a for-profit company with a social mission. When thinking about which strategies make the most sense donors should choose the ones that best reflect their appetite for financial risk, their beliefs about social change, and the impact they are seeking to generate.

The following strategies are meant to be a starting point for conversations with your clients. There is more information available about each of the options in other sections in this book as well as in *The Charitable Planning Desk Reference® for Advisors.*

◆ *Grantmaking*: The practice of giving money to support nonprofit organizations to support general operating expenses, specific programs, or capacity-building needs.

◆ *Program-Related Investing*: PRIs are vehicles for making inexpensive capital available to organizations that are addressing social or environmental concerns. Unlike grants, PRIs are expected to be repaid, often with at least a modest rate of return. Many use this strategy to complement and leverage traditional grantmaking.

◆ *Socially Responsible Investing:* Financial investment decision-making that takes into account a company's environmental, social, and governance (ESG) policies and records.

◆ *Impact Investing:* The intentional use of investment capital in for-profit social enterprises to create positive social and environmental outcomes. The investor has the expectation of a traditional financial return but also seeks a societal benefit.

Excerpted from *The Charitable Planning Desk Reference® for Advisors* 4th Edition.
© Strategic Philanthropy, Ltd. 2017–2018

What to Think about When Considering Cross-Border Giving

Before delving into cross-border giving, consider what you and/or your clients know about the places and issues they are interested in supporting. What assumptions and preconceived ideas inform their understanding of your interest areas? Encourage clients to take time to listen, learn, and assess their options before they act, especially if they are engaging in cross-border giving in response to an emergency. In the long run, a deeper knowledge about the issues and careful selection of appropriate partners will lead to greater peace of mind and greater potential success with your clients' giving.

Mitigating risk: Many risks, perceived or real, may be associated with cross-border giving. One major potential risk would be supporting a group that is laundering funds or otherwise directing monies to illegitimate entities. To be best equipped to avoid such risks, donors and their advisors should seek reliable experts who have relationships with, and expertise in, the countries where funds would be directed.

To mitigate risk, donors need to be aware of the restrictions on international grantmaking made since the PATRIOT Act was first passed in 2001. Information about how to conduct appropriate and necessary due diligence is discussed in **Chapter Seven**.

Accountability: Who is ultimately responsible for the good stewardship of the donation? Will it be the local nonprofit, an intermediary organization, or a US-based organization? It is important to clarify who is taking responsibility for the grant—who is directly accountable.

There is another kind of accountability: to the recipient of a charitable donation and their stakeholders. Can they depend on a donor's sustained interest even after the headlines have shifted to a new priority, trend, or crisis? Can they expect transparency and partnership with open dialogue and thoughtful engagement? Is the donor in for the *long haul* or is this a one-time donation? Have you been clear about your intentions and understand their expectations?

Cross-Cultural Competency: Working effectively across cultures is not always self-evident. It requires explicit policies and practices that follow an intentional set of principles and ethics to guide that work. Does the prospective organization demonstrate its ability to follow a set of beliefs and practices with integrity that respect and honor different cultural norms? Has the organization established a reputable track record of cultural fluency and respect? Do their actions demonstrate that they practice what they preach? *Do no harm* is an oft-cited phrase—here it carries particular weight, as cross-border giving can be riddled with often harmful yet unintended consequences.

A housing project gets derailed by local land ownership laws; a shoe or clothing donation project puts local cobblers and tailors out of work; water projects are installed without training for plumbers, etc. By understanding the local context and respecting the expertise that thrives in all parts of the world, you will get closer to a suitable level of cultural competency, and a more successful investment in the country in the end.

Because it is difficult to navigate the changing political and social issues, and since distance makes it hard to gather necessary qualifying information, it is often best to make donations through intermediaries. They not only have a deep knowledge of the issue areas but also of resources on the ground that work with them and their donors. Intermediaries offer a service that eliminates the need for donors to have to do deep research or address important due diligence issues.

There are various ways in which a donor can create partnerships with organizations: by making a donation to a large multi-national organization like CARE, Oxfam, or the Red Cross; by establishing a donor advised fund (DAF) with a nonprofit that partners with communities around the world; or by supporting a local organization that works directly with international partners.

Whatever way a donor wants to work in the global philanthropy arena, it's important to ensure that they have the cultural competency, appropriate legal status, and programming priorities aligned with the donor's interests. This will ensure a productive and rewarding partnership.

Impact

It can be challenging to feel connected to international grantmaking, and even more challenging to feel as though you have played a part in the success of an effort. Thoughtful and engaged donors who have done their research about the sector, country, and issues, will be better informed on the incremental steps needed to achieve the overall goals. Be patient, flexible, give credit where credit is due; respect and honor the work of those on the frontlines and be willing to get engaged for the long run. That is how impact will happen.

Whether you are focused on domestic issues or global concerns, *the Fundamental Keys to Successful Philanthropy* remain the same:

- ◆ Keep it simple and effective
- ◆ Commit to listening and learning
- ◆ Secure advisors and colleagues
- ◆ Know the rules of the road
- ◆ Have fun and trust your intuition

Susan Winer

Susan Winer is Chief Operating Officer of Strategic Philanthropy, Ltd., and a cofounder of the donor-centric philanthropic advisory firm headquartered in Chicago with offices in Detroit, MI.

Susan brings a unique skill set resulting from almost twenty-five years of work with established nonprofits and closely held businesses. As part of her focus on the family business and institutional services side of the firm's service offerings, she has led the development of the firm's Trusted Advisor training and education program that ensures a deeper understanding of how to undertake and support impactful philanthropy.

Susan is a prolific writer. She writes a monthly article for *Family Wealth Report* on philanthropy. She has authored or coauthored articles for such publications as: *PAM* (Private Asset Management), *Alliance*, *Family Business*, *STEP* (Society of Trust and Estate Practitioners), *Family Office Review*, The American Endowment Foundation, *Family Firm Institute*, and *Desert Charities*. She has also served on the faculty of the *Institute for Preparing Heirs* and has been a presenter at numerous workshops and conferences.

Susan has a BA from Wayne State University, attended graduate school at the University of Michigan, and successfully completed the mediation program at the Center for Mediation Law in California.

Betsy Brill

Betsy Brill is cofounder and President of Strategic Philanthropy, Ltd., a global philanthropic advisory firm. In 2000, after twenty years of working with foundations and nonprofit organizations, Betsy, along with Susan Winer, established Strategic Philanthropy, Ltd. This Multi-family Philanthropic Office® offers a wide range of support from strategy to implementation to back-office administration for foundations to HNW individuals, families, and family-owned businesses who want a more thoughtful and measurable approach to their lifetime and legacy giving.

Betsy has an MBA from Thunderbird School of Management and a Certificate in Nonprofit Management from Roosevelt University. She is a Trustee at Adler University, one of a select group of professionals designated as a National Center for Family Philanthropy Trained Consultant, and a registered Trust and Estate Practitioner (TEP) through the Society of Trust and Estate Practitioners (STEP). Betsy was also the only US member of STEP's Philanthropy Special Interest Group.

She has been a featured speaker at numerous conferences, including *Financial Advisor* magazine's annual Invest in Women Conference. She has authored numerous articles including pieces for the *Journal of Practical Estate Planning*, *Alliance Magazine*, *STEP Journal* (Society of Trust and Estate Practitioners), *Essentials Magazine*, and Adler University.

Chapter Twelve: Donor Perspectives

Part Two: Corporations as Donors

Deirdre White and Amanda McArthur

There is ongoing conversation about how donors can be increasingly strategic in their grantmaking to help the organizations they support achieve maximum impact and in turn, multiply the impact to the communities served. Grant monies targeted at programming can only go so far, due to operational constraints. This limits the ability of grantees to operate as efficiently as possible. Further, many grants are restricted to only support direct programming or provide minimal coverage for overall organizational operations. How then are nonprofits supposed to enhance their own administration? Even the most well-meaning organization will struggle to maintain the highest level of operations when forced to choose between self-improvement and serving their community.

Employee Volunteer Programs

There is a way, however, to support both direct programming and organizational capacity building at an incremental additional cost—but with a significantly enhanced return. Companies such as JPMorgan Chase include pro bono consulting as a component of their strategy. Through these employee volunteer programs, companies provide not only direct grant funds, but also an in-kind donation of organizational development consulting. This support, provided through a company's employees, comes at no financial cost to the grantee. Participating employees work on projects, engaging their professional skills to meet a direct and urgent need of the grantee organization. Projects can range from conducting feasibility studies for new service offerings to restructuring entire financial management systems to developing fundraising campaigns, among others.

The Benefits of Employee Volunteer Programs

Organizations receiving assistance are not alone in benefiting from employee volunteer programs—participating corporate employees and their sponsoring companies benefit as well. Employees develop their professional skills by applying them in a new context. Those who have participated in these programs report being more likely to stay with their current employer, and an increase in highly needed soft skills such as leadership, communications, and teamwork.[156]

As for the host organization, even short-term engagements with corporate employee volunteers have the potential to build organizational capacity for nonprofits. Organizations that host corporate volunteers serving as pro bono consultants see returns not only in the concrete deliverables but in a number of what we call the "-tions":

◆ *Acceleration*: Having surge support from corporate volunteers, even for just a relatively short period, enables the hosting organizations to drive forward a project more quickly than would have been the case without the intervention.

◆ *Reevaluation*: An influx of external ideas and perspective often prompts the host organizations to take a close and critical look at the organization, its mission and how it can best serve its purpose.

◆ *Integration*: We can no longer think of the public sector and the private sector as siloed from one another. To address the most complex challenges in society, it will take the public and private sectors not only working alongside one another, but directly in partnership. Employee volunteer programs provide an avenue to build these kinds of cross-sector bridges at the human level.

◆ *Optimization*: Due to resource constraints, nonprofit organizations often must prioritize providing services to their beneficiaries over improving their own internal processes—forcing them to be reactive to external pressures rather than proactively addressing them. Pro bono consultants from the private sector are often

---

[156] *IBM Corporate Service Corps: Impact Report 2016*, IBM, accessed August 28, 2017, *ibm.com*; *PULSE Volunteer Partnership: 2015 Annual Impact Report*, GSK, accessed August 28, 2017, *gsk.com*.

able to quickly assess and reformulate operations, ensuring that more time and resources can directly benefit the community as opposed to organizational administration.

◆ *Human Transformation*: Often nonprofit organizations struggle to keep the highest level of talent—in many cases because of a restricted ability to provide the type of professional development opportunities that lead to advancement and growth. While employee volunteer programs absolutely serve as a service learning opportunity for corporate employees, they can serve a similar purpose for the host organization's employees who work with and learn from the pro bono consultants.

Linking Employee Volunteer Program and Grantmaking: An Example

JPMorgan Chase established a program linking an infusion of human capital to financial grants. Though it is now a global program, sending teams of employees to multiple cities around the world for three-week pro bono assignments, the JPMorgan Chase Service Corps originally launched in 2014 in conjunction with JPMorgan Chase's $100 million commitment to revitalize the city of Detroit. By coupling their employees' talents with traditional grants, the company is further highlighting its commitment to the success of the city and the organizations that drive much-needed change at the grassroots level. As an executive from Eastern Market—a participating organization—noted, "The Detroit Service Corps took three years of my personal analysis of the wholesale market and not only elevated it, they validated it. When we construct the new food terminal, forty to fifty businesses in the district will now have a modern, food safety compliant, logistically efficient facility where they can conduct business."

As of October 2017, seven teams of up to sixteen JPMorgan Chase employees have each spent three weeks working with four organizations in Detroit. Each host organization is also a grantee of JPMorgan Chase—meaning there is a close relationship between the entities. In the case of JPMorgan Chase, many of the grantee organizations focus on community and/or workforce development—two of the pillars of the company's Corporate Responsibility strategy. Participating in the program exposes employees to critical issue areas and allows them to better understand challenges inherent to the nonprofit sector, while providing much-needed capacity-building support. This, in turn, enables more efficient utilization of grant monies. As Tara Cardone, Head of Employee Engagement and Volunteerism for JPMorgan Chase, notes, "Skills-based volunteerism offers another way to strengthen our relationships with nonprofit partners and double down on our philanthropic giving. By using JPMorgan Chase's most important asset—the expertise and commitment of our people—we help our nonprofit partners in Detroit and other cities increase their impact and ability to serve local communities."

Employee Matching Gift Programs

As we noted above, employees are often considered a company's best resource and many larger companies choose to offer employee matching gift programs as a way to build employee engagement. In these programs, usually a company will match an employee's charitable gift dollar-for-dollar (though some have been known to double or triple an employee's contribution). These pooled funds (the employee's gift and the company's matched amount) are then granted out to the recipient organization.

Many companies provide lists to employees which they can subsequently browse and choose the preferred recipient organization(s). Other companies let employees have free rein in their choice or will say that the organization needs to be a 501(c)(3) or reside in a country where the company operates. Still other companies will allow the employee to select as a recipient of their gift the organization with which they have been volunteering.

Though procedures vary across companies, employee matching gifts are a powerful way to motivate employees and leverage additional resources for nonprofit partners.

Four Ways to Link Human Capital, Grantmaking, and Employee Matching Gifts

The multiplier effect of linking human and financial capital contributions should not be overlooked. While many organizations are able to drive forward projects on their own without external support, human capital can create significant efficiencies that translate into greater impact in the community. Conversely, employee volunteer programs as standalone, in-kind support can indeed be transformational for an organization that is well-placed to drive forward any recommendations. However, some organizations, especially those at the very grassroots level (those that benefit most from the skills and expertise of the pro bono consultants) are unable to implement or sustain recommendations because of a lack of financial capital. By linking financial and human capital, companies like JPMorgan Chase are eliminating these constraints, improving community impact, and developing their next generation of leadership through service learning projects.

If linking your corporate employee engagement or leadership development efforts and grantmaking[157] is of interest, there are a number of initial steps we recommend you can take:

1. Examine your grantmaking portfolio to understand the internal capacity needs of your grantees. Do your corporate employees bring skills to the table that will benefit the grantee and their operations?

2. Speak with your corporate leadership. The most effective employee volunteer programs take employees away from their day jobs for at least some time, though not necessarily three weeks like the JPMorgan Chase Service Corps. Is this a feasible model for you? What human resource challenges might an employee volunteer program address?

3. Work with an intermediary organization—developing employee volunteer projects does require a specialized skillset in understanding what can be delivered in the time allotted, how to best utilize the skills of the corporate employees, and how to measure the impact of the interventions.

4. Consider how you might align your employee matching gift program to an organization that is receiving pro bono and philanthropic support. Employees are actively seeking opportunities to link purpose with their profession. Employee matching gifts with organizations being holistically supported by a company only serves to increase employee engagement.[158]

---

[157] While corporations provide donations and grants are issued by either the corporate foundation (if applicable) or by an intermediary organization supporting the corporation's philanthropic strategies, for the purpose of this chapter we use the term in its broader, less technical sense as to mean funding.

[158] Amanda MacArthur, "The Year That Purpose Drives Talent," *The Huffington Post*, 2017, *huffingtonpost.com*.

Deirdre White

Deirdre White is a globally recognized leader in building tri-sector partnerships to address the world's most pressing challenges. As CEO of the international NGO, PYXERA Global, she has led the transformation of the organization to one that maximizes impact through strong and strategic partnerships.

Deirdre's work has been featured in *Fortune, Wall Street Journal, Council on Foreign Relations*, and *Stanford Social Innovation Review*. She has been quoted in *Bloomberg, Forbes, Fast Company*, and *The Huffington Post*, and has been an invited speaker to TEDx, U.S. Department of State's Global Partnership Week, Shared Value Leadership Summit, and *Wall Street Journal's* CFO Network. Deirdre is a member of the MIT Ideas Global Challenge Advisory Board and the Bretton Woods Committee, and is an alumna of the Aspen Institute's Socrates Program.

Deirdre drives the discussion of new strategies for global engagement. She has served for multiple years as regional judge for the HULT Prize, a competition dedicated to launching the world's next wave of social entrepreneurs. Previously, Deirdre was cofacilitator of the Clinton Global Initiative's Employee Engagement Action Network. She also participated in The Rockefeller Foundation's renowned Bellagio Initiative and the Johnson Foundation at Wingspread's Leadership Forum for Global Citizen Diplomacy.

Amanda MacArthur

Amanda MacArthur is the Chief Program Officer at PYXERA Global, an international NGO that leverages the unique strengths of the public, private, and social sectors to address complex global challenges. Amanda leads a dedicated and passionate team to design, implement, and measure the impact of an array of programs that engage the power of tri-sector partnerships to address the most pressing challenges we face today.

Prior to her current role, Amanda built the organization's global *pro bono* practice, which is dedicated to building the capacity of social mission-driven organizations around the world by delivering more than $10 million in *pro bono* consulting annually. Amanda led IBM's first-ever Corporate Service Corps team in 2008 and has since developed similar programs for FedEx, The Dow Chemical Company, and Medtronic, among several other Fortune 500 companies.

She has written and spoken extensively on the power of global *pro bono* and experiential learning programs to transform how corporations interact with underserved markets while transferring much-needed skills and expertise to social mission-driven organizations. In addition to being recognized as among BMW Foundation Responsible Leaders, she is a member of the Bretton Woods Committee and is on the Leadership Faculty at Points of Light's Corporate Institute.

Appendix A

International Organizations Designated by Executive Order

African Development Bank (EO 12403, Feb. 8, 1983)

African Development Fund (EO 11977, Mar. 14, 1977)

Asian Development Bank (EO 11334, Mar. 7, 1967)

Caribbean Organization (EO 10983, Dec. 30, 1961)

Commission for the Study of Alternatives to the Panama Canal (EO 12567, Oct. 2, 1986)

Criminal Police Organization (EO 12425, June 16, 1983)

Customs Cooperation Council (EO 11596, June 5, 1971)

European Space Research Organization (EO 11760, Jan. 17, 1974)

Food and Agriculture Organization, The (EO 9698, Feb. 19, 1946)

Great Lakes Fishery Commission (EO 11059, Oct. 23, 1962)

Inter-American Defense Board (EO 10228, Mar. 26, 1951)

Inter-American Development Bank (EO 10873, Apr. 8, 1960)

Inter-American Institute for Cooperation on Agriculture (EO 9751, July 11, 1946)

Inter-American Investment Corporation (EO 12567, Oct. 2, 1986)

Inter-American Statistical Institute (EO 9751, July 11, 1946)

Inter-American Tropical Tuna Commission (EO 11059, Oct. 23, 1962)

Intergovernmental Committee for European Migration (formerly the Provisional Intergovernmental Committee for the Movement of Migrants from Europe) (EO 10335, Mar. 28, 1952)

Intergovernmental Maritime Consultative Organization (EO 10795, Dec. 13, 1958)

International Atomic Energy Agency (EO 10727, Aug. 31, 1957)

International Bank for Reconstruction and Development (EO 9751, July 11, 1946)

International Centre for Settlement of Investment Disputes (EO 11966, Jan. 19, 1977)

International Civil Aviation Organization (EO 9863, May 31, 1947)

International Coffee Organization (EO 11225, May 22, 1965)

International Committee of the Red Cross (EO 12643, June 23, 1988)

International Cotton Advisory Committee (EO 9911, Dec. 19, 1947)

International Development Association (EO 11966, Jan. 19, 1977)

International Fertilizer Development Center (EO 11977, Mar. 14, 1977)

International Finance Corporation (EO 10680, Oct. 2, 1956)

International Food Policy Research Institute (EO 12359, Apr. 22, 1982)

International Hydrographic Bureau (EO 10769, May 29, 1958)

International Institute for Cotton (EO 11283, May 27, 1966)

International Joint Commission--United States and Canada (EO 9972, June 25, 1948)

International Labor Organization, The (functions through staff known as The International Labor Office) (EO 9698, Feb. 19, 1946)

International Maritime Satellite Organization (EO 12238, Sept. 12, 1980)

International Monetary Fund (EO 9751, July 11, 1946)

International Pacific Halibut Commission (EO 11059, Oct. 23, 1962)

International Secretariat for Volunteer Service (EO 11363, July 20, 1967)

International Telecommunication Union (EO 9863, May 31, 1947)

International Telecommunications Satellite Organization (EO 11718, May 14, 1973)

International Wheat Advisory Committee (EO 9823, Jan. 24, 1947)

Multilateral Investment Guarantee Agency (EO 12647, Aug. 2, 1988)

Multinational Force and Observers (EO 12359, Apr. 22, 1982)

Organization for European Economic Cooperation (EO 10133, June 27, 1950) (now known as the Organization for Economic Cooperation and Development; 28 FR 2959, Mar. 26, 1963)

Organization of African Unity (EO 11767, Feb. 19, 1974)

Organization of American States (includes Pan American Union) (EO 10533, June 3, 1954)

Pacific Salmon Commission (EO 12567, Oct. 2, 1986)

Pan American Health Organization (includes Pan American Sanitary Bureau) (EO 10864, Feb. 18, 1960)

Preparatory Commission of the International Atomic Energy Agency (EO 10727, Aug. 31, 1957)

Preparatory Commission for the International Refugee Organization and its successor, the International Refugee Organization (EO 9887, Aug. 22, 1947)

South Pacific Commission (EO 10086, Nov. 25, 1949)

United International Bureau for the Protection of Intellectual Property (EO 11484, Sept. 29, 1969)

United Nations (EO 9698, Feb. 19, 1946)

United Nations Educational, Scientific, and Cultural Organization (EO 9863, May 31, 1947)

United Nations Industrial Development Organization (EO 12628, Mar. 8, 1988)

Universal Postal Union (EO 10727, Aug. 31, 1957)

World Health Organization (EO 10025, Dec. 30, 1948)

World Intellectual Property Organization (EO 11866, June 18, 1975)

World Meteorological Organization (EO 10676, Sept. 1, 1956)

World Tourism Organization (EO 12508, Mar. 22, 1985)

Appendix B

AFFIDAVIT FOR FOREIGN OR NON-US ORGANIZATIONS

AFFIDAVIT FOR: _____
(Complete legal name of organization. Type or print clearly)

Hereafter referred to in this Affidavit as the "Organization".

I, the undersigned, am making this Affidavit to assist (GRANTOR) and other grant-making foundations in the United States of America in determining whether the Organization is the equivalent of an exempt organization and public charity as defined in Sections 501(c)(3) and 509(a)(1), (2), or (3) of the United States Internal Revenue Code.

I. Principal. My name is _____
(Name of the principal officer or director signing this Affidavit)

I am the _____ of the Organization.
(Title of the principal officer or director signing this Affidavit)

II. Authorization. I am authorized by the Organization's governing body to make these declarations and to sign this affidavit and submit other supporting documents on behalf of the Organization as legally binding documents.

III. Formation and Purposes. The Organization was created in _____
(Year)

Under the laws of _____
(Identify country)

By _____ and is structured as a
(Identify statute, charter or other document)

_____
(Corporation, trust, association, government chartered entity, etc.)

IV. Exempt Purposes. The organization is organized and operated exclusively for one or more of the following purposes ("exempt purposes") as set forth in the United States Internal Revenue Code Section 501(c)(3).

(Check all boxes that apply)

❏ Charitable   ❏ Literary   ❏ Prevention of cruelty to children or animals under the laws of the country identified above

❏ Religious   ❏ Educational   ❏ Testing for public safety

❏ Scientific   ❏ Fostering national or international amateur sports competition

V. Program and Activities. I have attached to this affidavit a separate statement describing all of the past, present, and planned programs and activities of the organization.

This is attached as: _____
(Name of attachment)

VI. Governing Documents. The Organization's formation, governing, and operating documents ("governing documents") and other supporting documents are attached and incorporated by reference to this affidavit. These documents are currently used by the Organization in its governance and management and are recognized to be valid and enforceable under the laws of the Country in which the Organization operates.

It is essential that you attach English language copies of your founding charter, by-laws, and other documents that your organization uses to govern itself. If translation poses a major problem or constraint to your organization, please consult with your contact person at the (GRANTOR).

❏ True   ❏ False

VII. Limitations on activities. The Organization's governing documents **or** the laws and customs that apply to your Organization (or both) do not permit the Organization to:

a. Except as an insubstantial part of its activities, engage in activities other than for religious, charitable, scientific, literary, educational purposes, test for public safety, foster national or international amateur sports (but only if no part of its activities involve the provision of athletic facilities or equipment), or for the prevention of cruelty to children or animals;

*Laws and Customs ❏   Governing Documents ❏   → If so, what section?

b. Except as an insubstantial part of its activities, to attempt to influence legislation; and

*Laws and Customs ❏   Governing Documents ❏   → If so, what section?

c. Participate in, or intervene in (including the publishing or distributing of statements), any political campaign on behalf of (or in opposition to) any candidate for public office.

*Laws and Customs ❑　　　Governing Documents ❑　→ If so, what section?

The Organization's governing documents **or** the laws and customs that apply to your organization require the Organization to:

d. Ensure that no part of its earnings inures to the benefit of any private shareholder or individual;

*Laws and Customs ❑　　　Governing Documents ❑　→ If so, what section?

VIII. No improper private benefit. The laws and customs that apply to the Organization **or** its governing documents do not permit any of its income or assets to be given to, distributed to, or applied for the benefit of, a private person or non-charitable organization other than (a) as part of the Organization's exempt purposes or activities; or (b) as payment of reasonable compensation for services provided to the Organization; or (c) as payment for the fair market value of property the Organization has purchased.

*Laws and Customs ❑　　　Governing Documents ❑　→ If so, what section?

IX. No proprietary interest in Organization. The Organization has no owners, shareholders, members, or other entities that have a proprietary interest or ownership claims for the income or assets of the Organization.

❑ True　　　❑ False

The statements above place restrictions or limitations on public charities' operations and activities consistent with those required of a U.S. exempt organization. It is important to understand that when you sign this Affidavit, you are saying that Items 6 through 9 are applicable for your organization. Please read these statements very carefully and indicate provisions, which, if any, apply or do not apply to your organization.

X. Related Organizations. An organization, including a nonprofit, nongovernmental organization, a stock corporation, a partnership or limited liability company, a trust, and a governmental unit or other government entity is a related organization if it stands, for any time during the Organization's fiscal year, in one or more of the following relationships to the applicant Organization: (a) "Parent" - an organization that controls the applicant Organization; (b) "Subsidiary" - an organization controlled by the applicant Organization; or (c) "Brother/Sister" - an organization that is controlled by the same person or persons that controls the applicant Organization.

Control is exercised by one or more persons (whether individuals or organizations) if they have the power to remove and replace (or to appoint or elect, if such power includes a continuing power to appoint or elect periodically or in the event of vacancies) a majority of the applicant Organization's directors, trustees, or governing body, or a majority of the members who have the power to elect a majority of the applicant Organization's directors, trustees, or governing body. Such power can be exercised directly by a (parent) organization through one or more of the (parent) organization's officers, directors, trustees, officers, or agents, acting in their capacity as officers, directors, trustees, officers, or agents of the (parent) organization. A (parent) organization controls a (subsidiary) nonprofit organization if a majority of the subsidiary's directors or trustees are trustees, directors, officers, employees, or agents of the parent.

Select the correct answer as it pertains to your organization. Explain in detail any formal relationship your organization has with another organization. Describe only those that control your organization, or are legally connected to your organization. If there is any uncertainty as to whether there is or may be a relationship between or among the applicant Organization and other entity, disclose and explain in detail the relationship.

The Organization is (*choose one*):

❑ Not operated or otherwise controlled in connection with any other related organization.

❑ Operated or otherwise controlled in connection with or by another related organization or organizations in the following manner. *(Describe fully on attached sheets)*

XI. Accounting year-end. The Organization's account (or fiscal) year-end is:
_____
(Specify month and day)

XII. Qualification as publicly supported organization. The Organization is *(select the one category that describes the Organization)*:

❑ A school (meaning an educational organization for which all of the following statements are TRUE - strike any statement that is FALSE):

    ❑ It normally maintains a regular facility and curriculum;

    ❑ It normally has a regular enrolled body of students in attendance at the place where its educational activities are regularly carried on; and

❑ It has adopted in its governing documents a nondiscriminatory policy which "admits students of any race, color, national and ethnic origin to all the rights, privileges, programs, and activities generally accorded or made available to students at the school. It does not discriminate on the basis of race, color, national and ethnic origin in administration of its educational policies, admissions policies, scholarship and loan programs, and athletic and other school administered programs." The school operates in accordance with this nondiscriminatory policy and publishes this policy annually to the general public. See generally, Rev. Rul. 71-447, 1971-2 C.B. 230, and Rev. Rul. 75-231, 1975-1 C.B. 158, and as implemented in Rev. Proc. 75-50, 1975-2 C.B. 587, which is explained in more detail in the General Instructions to IRS Form 5578.

❑ A hospital (that is, an organization whose principal purpose or function is the providing of medical or hospital care). If the hospital's principal purpose or function is providing medical education or medical research, it means that the hospital is actively engaged in providing medical or hospital care to patients on its premises or in its facilities, on an inpatient or outpatient basis, as an integral part of its medical education or medical research functions.

❑ A church (that is, a church, synagogue, temple, mosque, or other formal place of worship).

❑ A governmental agency (*describe*) _____

_____

_____

❑ None of the above, but it satisfies a public support test as demonstrated by the attached schedule of financial support for the five most recently completed taxable years.

XIII. Distribution of assets on dissolution. These provisions apply in the event the nonprofit organization stops its work, ceases to exist, or must otherwise dissolve or liquidate its assets. Attach English translations of the governing document and statutes that control the distribution of your assets upon liquidation, if not already provided under Item 4 above. *(Check one and supply the required attachment(s)).*

❑ In the event the Organization ceases to operate or is to be liquidated or dissolved, **the Organization's governing documents** requires that **all** of the Organization's remaining assets shall be distributed to another nonprofit or nongovernmental organization for one or more exempt purposes to include religious, charitable, scientific, literary, educational purposes, test for public safety, foster national or international sports amateur sports (but only if no part of its activities involve the provision of athletic facilities or equipment), or for the prevention of cruelty to children or animals.

I have attached (in English) a copy of the governing instruments or provisions in the Organization's governing instruments that control the distribution of its assets on dissolution or liquidation.

The relevant provisions are located in _____

(Identify section where relevant dissolution provisions are to be found)

❑ In the event the Organization ceases to operate or is to be liquidated or dissolved, **the statutory law** governing the Organization require that **all** of the Organization's remaining assets shall be distributed to another nonprofit or nongovernmental organization for one or more exempt purposes to include religious, charitable, scientific, literary, educational purposes, test for public safety, foster national or international sports amateur sports (but only if no part of its activities involve the provision of athletic facilities or equipment), or for the prevention of cruelty to children or animals.

I have attached (in English) a copy of the statutory law which controls the distribution of the organization's assets on dissolution or liquidation.

XIV. Binding representations. The representations and statements made in this Affidavit are binding on the Organization and its officers, directors, trustees, and governing body.

I swear or affirm under penalties of perjury under the laws of the United States of America, to the best of my knowledge and belief, that the foregoing and statements and representations and all supporting documents which are attached and submitted in support of this Affidavit are complete, true, and correct as of this date.

This the _____ day of _____, 20_____.

By:

_____
(Authorized signature)

_____
(Print name)

_____
(Print title)

Country/Province _____

Nation _____

_____
(Notary Public)

This the _____ day of _____, 20_____.

(Notary Seal)

Attachments:

*(Delete references to documents not attached. List here documents that are actually attached, and give each an identifying number. **Please affix a corresponding number to the attached documents.**)*

1. Description of programs and activities

2. Copies (in English) of the charter, by-laws, and other documents that govern the organization

3. Public Support Schedule

Appendix C

Sample Grant Agreement

On behalf of (GRANTEE), hereby "the Organization", I agree that any funds (GRANTOR) may grant to the Organization during its Eligibility Period (defined below) will be used as follows:

◆ The Grants, any income earned on Grant funds, and any capital assets created, developed, or acquired with the Grant funds will be used only for charitable purposes, specifically to fund the charitable activities described in the proposed project and only for expenses incurred after the payment of this grant.

◆ The Organization will provide (GRANTOR) with annual written reports, signed by an officer of the Organization, describing its use of the Grants provided by (GRANTOR) each fiscal year. Such written reports will discuss the Organization's compliance with the terms of the Grants, the progress made in accomplishing the purposes of the outstanding Grants during that fiscal year, and any changes to the information submitted in this agreement. Such reports shall be due 4 months after the end of the Organization's fiscal year. (GRANTOR) will continue to collect a report for each fiscal year thereafter in which the Organization has unexpended funds from the Grants. (GRANTOR) reserves the right to modify this reporting schedule.

◆ The Organization shall only report on expenditures related to (GRANTOR) grant funds. Expenditures from other grantors should not be included on grantee reports submitted to (GRANTOR).

◆ The Organization will not use the Grants, directly or indirectly:

❖ to carry on any propaganda or otherwise attempt to influence legislation;

❖ to influence the outcome of any specific public election or to carry on any voter registration drive;

❖ to induce or encourage violations of law or public policy or to cause any improper private benefit to occur;

❖ to provide tuition, medical expenses, or other economic benefits to a donor, a donor's advisor, or a member of a donor's family;

❖ or to take any other action inconsistent with Section 501(c)(3) of the Internal Revenue Code.

◆ The Organization does not knowingly employ individuals or contribute funds to organizations that the Organization otherwise knows to support terrorism or to individuals or organizations found on any terrorist-related list promulgated by the US Government, the United Nations or the European Union, including the Department of Treasury's Office of Foreign Assets Control Specially Designated Nationals List, the Department of Justice's Terrorist Exclusion List and the list annexed to Executive Order 13224.

◆ The Organization warrants that it does not and will not use Grant funds to (i) make any illegal payments directly or indirectly to government officials, political parties, or political candidates outside the US, (ii) make any other payments to such persons (or to others knowing that they will use the funds to make payments to such persons) that would cause (GRANTOR) or any other person to violate the United States Foreign Corrupt Practices Act of 1977 as amended.

◆ The Organization will maintain records of receipts and expenditures of the Grant funds for a period of seven years after the Grant funds have been expended. The Organization will make such records available to (GRANTOR) for inspection, upon request. (GRANTOR) may monitor and conduct an evaluation of operations under the Grants, which may include a site visit arranged by (GRANTOR) to observe the Organization's program, discuss the program with the Organization's personnel and review financial records and other materials connected with the activities financed by the Grants. If (GRANTOR) is not satisfied with the quality of the work done or the progress made under the Grants, or determines that the Organization is not capable of satisfactorily completing the Grants, (GRANTOR) may, in its sole discretion, withhold payment of Grant funds, or declare the Grants terminated.

◆ If the Organization is dissolved, if the Grants are terminated, or if the Organization is otherwise unable to use the Grants for the activities described in the proposed project, the Organization will promptly return any unexpended grant funds to (GRANTOR).

◆ The Organization and its authorized signatory certify that the responses to this Grant Eligibility Application are true and complete. If they are not, (GRANTOR) may declare the Grants terminated and require repayment of some or all of the Grants.

◆ If any portion of the Grants is used for any purpose other than those described in the proposed project, the Organization will promptly notify (GRANTOR). (GRANTOR) will withhold any further payment of Grant funds until it has received assurance that the Organization has taken appropriate precautions sufficient to prevent future misuse from occurring. In addition, (GRANTOR) may require the Organization to repay some or all of the Grant funds.

◆ The Eligibility Period ceases, and this agreement shall be considered terminated, two-three years after the parties execute this agreement, except to the extent (GRANTOR) extends or shortens such eligibility period (and this agreement) in its own discretion. The Organization represents, warrants, and undertakes that the facts stated in this GEA, and such updates to those facts that the Organization may submit from time to time in subsequent communications with (GRANTOR), are accurate and complete.

◆ The Organization acknowledges and accepts that the award of any Grant is a matter of (GRANTOR's) sole and absolute discretion and that nothing in the project proposal, these Grant Terms or any prior dealings with (GRANTOR), imposes any obligation on (GRANTOR) to award any Grants. In particular, the Organization acknowledges that execution of these Grant Terms by (GRANTOR) merely indicates agreement and acceptance by (GRANTOR) that a necessary pre-condition to the award of any Grants (namely the agreement and acceptance by the Organization of these Grant Terms) has been satisfied.

◆ The Organization understands that this Agreement does not confer upon the Organization any special recognition from, endorsement by, or affiliation with (GRANTOR).

◆ (GRANTOR) reserves the right to change these Grant Terms in the future, and such terms shall become binding upon the Organization if it does not object within 30 days after receiving notice of such changes. If the Organization objects and the parties cannot agree on suitable terms within 30 days, the Grants will terminate.

◆ This Agreement is governed by the laws of the (INSERT STATE) and, with respect to the Grants, supersedes all prior agreements of the parties.

PLEASE SIGN BELOW. UNSIGNED GRANT AGREEMENTS CANNOT
BE ACCEPTED.

Agreed and Accepted (GRANTEE):

by _____ its _____ on _____
      AUTHORIZED   POSITION OF   DATE
      SIGNATURE   SIGNATORY

Agreed and Accepted: (GRANTOR)

by _____ its _____ on _____
      AUTHORIZED   POSITION OF   DATE
      SIGNATURE   SIGNATORY

Appendix D

Sample Grantee Report Form

For all grants received between [DATE] and [DATE]

Grantee: [GRANTEE NAME]

Address:

[ADDRESS 1]

[ADDRESS 2]

[CITY]

[STATE]

[PROVINCE]

[ZIP]

[COUNTRY]

Grant(s) received from [YOUR ORGANIZATION] [DATE] AND [DATE]

Date (mm/dd/yyyy)	Amount US	Amount FX	Currency Type	Grant Purpose
Total				

PLEASE COMPLETE ALL QUESTIONS. ATTACH ADDITIONAL PAGES AS NECESSARY. PLEASE REMEMBER TO SIGN THE LAST PAGE.

1. Please confirm the end date of your organization's fiscal year: _____

2. Has the entirety of the grant(s) been expended? [Please circle one]
   Yes   **No**

If you answered **No**, please explain when and how the remaining funds are expected to be spent.

3. Were any funds utilized to purchase Capital Assets? This would include anything that was purchased or constructed that is now recorded as an asset in your financial statements. If so, please provide information on the purchase, the amount expended and the benefit to your organization.

4. Please describe the purpose and activities for which grant funds were expended. If you received more than [AMOUNT] from [YOUR ORGANIZATION] last year: please provide a brief breakdown of how the funds were expended.

5. What has been the outcome or impact of the [YOUR ORGANIZATION'S] grant(s)? What (if any) measurable difference has the grant(s) made for your organization and/or those served by the grant(s)? Please provide quantifiable results of this grant, if possible.

6. What lessons did you learn? If you were unable to accomplish or make any progress on your intended grant purpose, how will you change your approach?

7. Did this project receive any press or news coverage? If available, please attach copies of clippings and/or photos with your report.

If any part of questions 1-7 is not applicable to your organization, please indicate why.

I certify that I am authorized to sign this report on behalf of the Grantee named above and that all grant funds listed above were expended for charitable purposes and no portion of the grant funds were diverted to non-charitable uses, the donor, the donor's family or donor advisor. Grantee asserts that it has complied with all of the terms and conditions specified in the Grantee Agreement with [YOUR ORGANIZATION].

By: _____   _____
              (signature)   (date)

_____   _____
           (printed name)   (title)

_____
                          (direct email address)

Appendix E

Timeline of Post 9/11 Anti-Terrorist Financing Laws and Evolution of Voluntary Guidelines

Annex to Chapter Nine, *Responsible Giving: the International Grantmakers' Perspective,* **Jane Peebles**

9/11/2001	Terrorist attacks on US soil.
9/25/2001	Then President George W. Bush signs Executive Order 13224, requiring maintenance of the Specially Designated Nationals List and authorizing freezing of assets of organizations supporting terrorism.
10/26/2001	Congress amends the USA PATRIOT Act, imposing stricter penalties for knowingly supporting terrorism.
11/2002	Department of the Treasury releases "Anti-Terrorist Financing Guidelines: Voluntary Best Practices for US Based Charities" (2002 Voluntary Guidelines).
5/2003	IRS Announcement 2003-29 requests comments on the 2002 Voluntary Guidelines and data about grantmaking procedures.
7/2003–8/2003	The Treasury Guidelines Working Group lodges comments on the 2002 Voluntary Guidelines.
4/2004	Treasury invites the nonprofit sector to propose alternatives to the 2002 Voluntary Guidelines for minimizing diversion of funds to terrorists.

3/2005	The TGWG proposes its "Principles of International Charity" as an alternative to the 2002 Voluntary Guidelines and asks Treasury to withdraw the 2002 Voluntary Guidelines.
12/5/2005	Treasury releases the draft 2005 revised Voluntary Guidelines and requests further comments.
9/29/2006	Treasury releases its third iteration of the Voluntary Guidelines.
12/18/2006	The TGWG again asks Treasury to withdraw the Voluntary Guidelines in favor of the "Principles of International Charity."
3/2007	Treasury releases its Risk Assessment Matrix.
11/2010	The TGWG formally terminates discussions with Treasury out of frustration.

Appendix F

Anti-Terrorist Financing Legislation and Guidelines

Annex to Chapter Nine, *Responsible Giving: the International Grantmakers' Perspective*, Jane Peebles

Watch Lists

◆ US Department of the Treasury's Office of Foreign Assets Control Specially Designated Nationals List (OFAC SDN)

◆ US Department of State Terrorist Exclusion List (TEL)

◆ Executive Order 13224 (original list)

◆ Executive Order 13224 (amended list)

◆ United Nations Security Council Resolution 1267 list

◆ European Union EU Regulation 2580 list

Further Reading on Anti-Terrorist Financing Rules

1. "Handbook on Counter-Terrorism Measures: What US Nonprofits and Grantmakers Need to Know," Independent Sector, Council on Foundations, and Day, Berry & Howard Foundation (3/15/04).

2. I.R.S. Announcement 2003-29, 2003-20 I.R.B. 928, regarding International Grant-Making and International Activities by Domestic 501(c)(3) organizations.

3. "Principles of International Charity," developed by the Treasury Guidelines Working Group of Charitable Sector Organizations and Advisors, a working group of over 40 charitable sector organizations under the leadership of the Council on Foundations (3/05).

Index

CPSIA information can be obtained
at www.ICGtesting.com
Printed in the USA
BVHW041152311218
536784BV00002B/2/P